VALUE EDUCATION
A STUDY OF PUBLIC OPINION

VALUE EDUCATION

A STUDY OF PUBLIC OPINION

By

K.L. Gandhi

Value Education
a Study of Public Opinion

ISBN : 978-81-212-0429-3

First Published 1993, reprint 2013 in India by
Gyan Publishing House
23, Main Ansari Road, Daryaganj,
New Delhi - 110002
Phones : 23282060, 23261060
Fax : (011) 23285914
E-mail: books@gyanbooks.com
website: gyanbooks.com

Printed at : Sagar Color Scan, New Delhi.

CONTENTS

Introduction

This book has no pretensions of being a pioneering work in the field of value-education. Numerous Committees and Commissions have reported on the promotion of moral values. Literature— ancient and modern — is replete with reference to the dissemination of values in the society. It is, therefore, possible that what has been said here may have been said before or elsewhere. One is, therefore, justified in questioning the desirability of this work and more so when we tend to consign even the best of reports to the cold storage rather than implementing the suggestions contained in these reports. If such pessimism had prevailed in the writer's mind the idea of this work would have been given up at the very embryonic stage itself. This work was undertaken with a faith that something in the nature of the views of a sizable sample of our population was lacking and was badly needed at the present juncture of the nation's moral crisis.

The Present Crisis :

Modern science has placed a proverbial Alladin's lamp in the hands of man. The jinn is at his command now. Man can order the jinn to annihilate the structure which his predecessors have taken several millennia to create or else ask him (the jinn) to usher in an era of prosperity in the world. The choice rests with the modern man; and in making a choice he will inevitably be guided by his sense of values. So the question of values becomes important.

This is an 'age of anxiety'. Mankind is sitting on an arsenal of nuclear and other weapons capable of mass destruction. If through miscalculation or over-enthusiasm or some self-generating phenomenon, these destructive weapons get unleashed, a ghastly catastrophe unparalleled in human history would ensue. Nuclear blasts would fill the atmosphere with smoke, soot, mounds of earth and dust. This would cut off sun's light and heat reaching the globe. It would usher in a prolonged spell of nuclear night and nuclear winter. The temperature on earth would fall to a sub-zero level and water would freeze. The protective layer of ozone in the atmosphere, which is already reported to have suffered a damage, would vanish and ultra violet rays would hit the earth. For years to come, radio activity would fill the atmosphere. All this would result in hitherto unknown diseases and take a heavy toll of vegetable and animal life. The after-effects of the holocaust are so frightening that some of the scientists feel that those who die with the first nuclear blast would be better off than the ones who survive it to suffer genetic mutations and many other concomitant consequencs.

'Political anxiety' is another phenomenon, which is manifest in national and international disputes. There is a spate of terrorists' activities encouraged by groups or nations against one another. There are the ethnic disputes which are getting multiplied rather than resolved and lastly there are problems of territorial adjustments, river-waters distribution and sometimes even over non-issues.

'Economic anxiety' emerges from monopolisation of resources by a few, at the level of the state or that of the individual. In a close-circuited, fast-shrinking and mutually-interacting world, economic imbalances and exploitation of the 'have-nots'; by the 'haves' is resulting in unrest and violence of varying dimensions.

The Hippie Movement, high rate of suicides, increase in husband-wife divorces and a large number of broken homes among the nations of the world demonstrate that wealth alone cannot buy mental peace, happiness, or contentment. Something more is to be searched for so that life becomes more worth living.

It is also an age of 'conflict'. The age of science and technology has aggravated this conflict manifold. To be secular or religious, to accept or to reject the tradition, to prefer cultural isolation or to allow cultural interaction are some of the dimensions of this conflict. Conflicts also arise, when an old code loses relevance or new values emerge. This occurs due to changes in the population graph, advancement of knowledge and technological vistas, or some other similar strongly influencing factors. Exploding population may call for new values like family-planning, reproduction by genetic selection (provided its misuse or horrible consequences can be avoided) and even a legislation such as 'reproduction only by those who are genetically suitable'.

With the progress of technology, there has been a continuous flow of population from the rural areas to the urban industrial centres. In the process of migration, group loyalties and consequently the value system of the migrants get temporarily or permanently disoriented. Resolution of conflict between the value systems, of different groups brought together by political, economic or other compulsions is necessary, if mankind is to live in peace and happiness.

At the global level, tne 'anxiety and conflict' have been sought to be lessened by setting up organisations like the United Nations, Non-Aligned Movement, Commonwealth of Nations and other regional or sub-regional associations and by signing various pacts; but conflicts continue and man's anxiety remains. Possibly, this state of affairs would continue till such time we identify the basic cause of the entire malaise rather than tinkering with externalities.

India has, in the past, made a substantial contribution to the evolution of mankind's culture and moral values. According to Encyclopaedia Britannica (Vol. 18, p. 630), the Vedas are the oldest philosophical literature and philosophical ethics of mankind. Numerous foreign travellers and writers of historical records have, from time to time, written in praise of the high standards of Indian morality. This contribution is as significant as that of modern Europe in the fields of secular science and technology. Today, man, with a power-house of knowledge at his command is in greater need of a cultural reorientation than he was at any time in the past. India may, therefore, be destined, once again, to lead mankind out of the present stage of multiple crises and more so of the moral crisis or the crisis of values which is at the root of all these crises.

Harvalth George Paloczi writes, "What most majorities have lacked during five thousand years of recorded history was not so much intellectual capacity as moral character. In the age of H bombs and other colossal man-made dangers, the need for a minimum standard of moral conduct should be obvious to every one, save some political leaders and the criminally insane.[1]

Though the need for value education has been felt and expressed for a long time in India, as in other parts of the world, precious little has been done in this regard by way of any specific action. No doubt, certain denominational educational institutions have provided in their curricula teaching of 'moral science' but no evidence is available to affirm that such teachings have led to improved moral standards. These moral-teachings are mostly limited to readings and sermons from some scriptures, possibly falling flat on the ears of disinterested listeners.

Methodology :

This work is based on a research study. Therfore, it would be appropriate to briefly allude to this research work and its methodology.

In order to determine the opinions of people, questionnaires given in Appendix IV and Appendix V, were prepared. These are respectively addressed to students and non-students (hereafter referred to as general population) of the Union Territory of Delhi.[2] While designing these questionnaires, the following main points were kept in view :

a) The language of the questionnaires should be easy and unambiguous.

b) Preference should be given to including statements on such ethical values, which are subject of greater concern to the society in the present-day context.

c) Different approaches were adopted while framing the questionnaires so that the chance of casual or inattentive ticking against the statements in one of the three columns can be minimised. A comparative study of statements 3, 7 and 13 in the questionnaire for students would explain this point.

d) Reaction of the respondents were invited on a three-point scale-agree, undecided and disagree. It was felt that in the research where the problem was intended to be studied in general terms and by a mixed group (by way of educational standards), three-point scale would be good enough.

e) Statements were included in the questionnaires on all major aspects of the problem which had been stipulated at the time of formulating the research proposal or even later on, such as the present status of values in the society, the urge for implementing programmes of value-education, curriculum and methodology of value-education and so on.

Although it was felt that certain terms in these questionnaires were likely to be interpreted differently by different people, it was not found feasible to incorporate precise definitions of these terms in the questionnaires. This applies also to the list of 84 values appended to these questionnaires. It was, however, made clear in the title of the study, as well as in the forwarding letter addressed to the respondents, that for purposes of the study, value-education was synonymous with moral education.

Data Collection

The questionnaires were given to the respondents personally or sent through mail or the local educational institutions. The note which contained instructions for the Principals of the educational institutions, who helped in getting the responses to the questionnaires from a large number of respondents can be seen at Appendix VI. Many school-students were given time during school hours to react to the questionnaire.

In all 1148 respondents reacted to the two questionnaires—881 respondents from the general public and 267 were school and college students. A category-wise break-up of the respondents is given in Appendices VII, VIII, IX and X. Of the questionnaires given or sent to respondents, over 50 per cent were received back after the respondents had done the needful.

Analysis and Presentation of the Data:

Data were collected and compiled on a three-point scale. Compilation of the data was got done through a computer agency. Information collected through the questionnaires was supplemented by interviews with selected respondents. Although reactions of 881 respondents in regard to all statements in the questionnaires were available in terms of their educational qualifications and professional status and that of school and college students separately, selective approach was adopted in presesnting the data so that the presentation does not become confusing.

Implementation:

Many reports and studies in India are consigned to the forgotten shelves without being implemented. Two very sharp reactions in this regard— one from a school student and the other from a college student—are reproduced below in order. Incidently, both these students are female.

(i) "If some action is taken on the basis of this questionnaire, then it is useful and beneficial, otherwise stop it".

(ii) "We have done this so many times in school also, but have as yet not got any fruitful result or seen any change in the society. I hope this will help in bringing about a change".

It is, therefore, essential that on the basis of all such research findings a suitable programme of implementation is drawn up so that the society has some return of its investment into such studies.

Areas of Future Research:

No study can be completely definitive, much less a subject of this type. There is always a scope for diversification in methodology and instrument. A study also throws up issues of significance which need further investigation. Some of the future areas of research in this field could be:

(1) The nature and extent of coordination between the formal, non-formal and informal education in the programme of value-education.

(2) Comparison of the success stories of the value-education programme under the capitalist and the socialist systems.

(3) Identifying in detail causes of the "moral degradation" in various sections of the society.

References and Notes

1. Horvalth George Paloczi; *Youth Up in Arms;* Weidenfeld and Nicolson, London, 1971; p.326.
2. The forwarding letter, the Personal Data sheet and the Appendix containing List of the Values in both the questionnaires were common, hence these have not been repeated. The words 'S' and 'G' on the first page of these questionnaires stand respectively 'for students' and 'for general populace'. Both the questionnaires contained English as well as Hindi versions. The respondents were free to give their comments in either of the languages— Hindi, English, or Urdu.

Morality-Conceptual Framework

Value-system and Morality are amorphous concepts. Time, place and social milieu are the chief determinants of all moral codes in the world. Morality, therefore, does not lend itself to any precise interpretation. A few examples would illustrate how man's attitude to moral values tends to change or develop along these variables.

Modern science holds that 'matter' is governed by the theory of *'cause and effect'*. Ancient philosophers had looked upon the phenomenon of cause and effect in a wider as well as different context. Indians extended the 'cause and effect' concept to human life-cycle and the world of spirit; and they called it the *'Principle of karma'*. According to this theory, the present state of every creature is the *summum bonum* of his or her past actions in the past and the present life. The Buddhists also subscribe to this view. Zend Avesta of the Zoroastrians (Parsees) holds that after death, the soul of a good person is met by a beautiful maiden, who says to him, "I am thy own conscience: I was lovely and thou madest me still lovlier; I was fair and thou madest me still fairer through thy good thought, thy good speech, and thy good deeds". And then the soul is led into the paradise of endless light. On the contrary, the soul of a wicked person is met by a hideous old woman,"uglier than the ugliest thing", who is his own conscience. She says to him, "I am thy bad actions. O youth of evil thoughts, of evil words, ot evil deeds, of evil religion, it is on account of thy will and actions that I am hedious and vile". Thereafter, the soul is led down into the hell of endless darkness.[1]

It is obvious that convictions of this nature will have a far-reaching effect on our thoughts, words and moral behaviour. However, there are many materialists who believe in cause and effect theory but who have no faith in a life after death. According to them, the five elements of air, earth, fire, sky and water, of which every creature on this earth is made up of,merge into the respective five elements of nature after death and this heralds the end of the life-cycle. Actions of such people are, obviously not conditioned by thoughts of 'life to come' and mans soul facing the consequences of his actions. Let us next consider some more specific examples in relation to varying social milieus.

The Zoroastrians declare 'truthfulness' as the highest virtue. The ancient Persians had a great veneration for truth and a strong punishment was provided for false swearing. Truthfulness, as a virtue, does not have that high place in Japan. This could also be due to the fact that the Japanese, in view of their great veneration for their superiors, could not say unpleasant things to them even if these were true. The Greeks, prior to Socrates, were reputed for their disregard for promises and truthfulness. They could practise fraud freely to achieve their end. It goes to the credit of Socrates to have tried to reverse this trend among the Greeks and finally having laid down his life for the ideal of truth.

The 'caste-system' among the Hindus, which was evolved as a division of labour and was nurtured by them for promoting specialisation in trade, industry and various professions among its adherants, stands condemned today by the Hindus themselves. With the cruelties perpetrated by the high-castes on the low-castes in the past, any discrimination based on caste is now a legal offence in India.

Worse than the caste-system was the custom of slavery which was commonly accepted by the Babylonians, the Romans, the Muslims and the Greeks. In fact, slavery is considered by the historians as an important contributory factor for the fall of the Roman civilisation. The master had an unquestioned authority over his slave; he gloated over the agony of his slave till the latter died. This kind of insensitivity to morality would, today, make anyone shiver to the marrow of his bone. According to Hobhouse, "the recognition of the slave traffic by Mohammedanism has been, and is to this day, a curse to Africa and a source of disturbance to the world's politics".[2]

Aristotle taught to hunt barbarians (all non-Greeks) for purposes of getting slaves and he considered it as right and proper as to hunt animals for food and sacrifice.[3]

Filial loyalty was at great premium in ancient China. A father, with the consent of the son's maternal uncle, could require a magistrate to whip to death his unfilial son. "A patricide is beheaded, his body cut in pieces, his house torn down, his neighbours are punished, his chief teacher is put to death, and the magistrates of the district in which he lived are degraded or deposed".[4] Filial piety and duty towards the emperor are the two corner-stones of the Japanese ethics. The latter would invite outright rejection by most modern nations today.

Roman Catholics, among Christians, regard celibacy as a virtue; but among the Zoroastrians celibacy, fasting and self-mortifications have no place. Islam goes to the extent of accepting and even justifying polygamy.[5]

For all followers of Christ, compassion is a laudable quality. The edifice of Jainism would crumble if the elements of compassion and non-violence are excluded from it. In contrast, the Hellas' motto for justice was 'Do no wrong, and suffer no wrong to self or others', with emphasis on the latter. The Hellas considered revenge a virtue if a person had been wronged. Forgiveness was considered a trait of a timid mind. Hammurabi's code of ethics in Babylon, which is considered to be one of the oldest in the world, recommended "eye for eye and tooth for tooth". If a person killed someone's daughter, the killer's daughter was butchered in retaliation and the society accepted it; It is a matter of conjecture what happened if the killer had no daughter !

The Chinese moralist Mencius called the war marshals as great criminals though one may find the present-day Communist China far removed from this thinking.

The war ethics of today is shrouded with hypocrisy. Today, every war is claimed to have been fought for peace and nuclear weapons are said to have been manufactured for self-defence only. The war ethics of our ancestors was, however, more straight-forward. In India war was assigned to low place. The king could keep an army and it was his duty to protect his people. Manu's laws of war forbade use of poisonous weapons, striking an enemy without armour or an onlooker civilian, or one who was asleep or unconscious, etc. War prisoners could be made to work;but they were to be given proper food. Special care was to be taken of children, women and the old people. And so on.[6] Militarism, in any form has no place in Buddhism. Contrary to this, the Assyrians and the Babylonians exulted over the cruelties perpetrated by them in wars. One such account is given below :

"The nobles, as many as had revolted, I flayed; with their skins I covered the pyramid. Some (of these) I immured in the midst of the pyramid; others above the pyramid I impaled on stakes—three thousand of their captives I burned with fire. I left no one alive among them to become a hostage— I cut off the hands (and) feet of some; I cut off the noses, the ears (and) the fingers of others; the eyes of numerous soldiers I put out. In the middle (of them) I suspended their heads on vine stemp in the neighbourhood of their city. Their young men (and) maidens I burned as a holocaust".[7]

The brief picture indicates the wide variations in the value-systems of different societies living at different times in the same or different geographical regions.

Transformation of Values : Some Causes:

Transformation of values takes place due to several factors—political, economic and social. In the political sphere, constitutionally and democratically elected governments have replaced the rule of the colonisers, the maharajas and the nawabs. The value-based politics of the days of yore de-facto stands condemned today by the political opportunists all over the world. In India too, the principled politics of Mahatma Gandhi, Jawahar Lal Nehru and Jaya Prakash Narain stands abandoned by most of the politicians.

In the sphere of economics, the mercantile industry has been replaced by modern industries bringing a new class of entrepreneurs with new values. The pursuit of heavy industries has led to heavy investments, higher production, consumerism and so on. It has also led to the concentration of capital in fewer hands. The gap between the rich and the poor in all countries as well as at the international levels has widened, leading to conflicts in several new forms between the rich and the poor. The urge to gain political supremacy in the world has led to the cold-war situation which is altogether a new concept.

In the social sphere, though casteism has been legally banned in India, it gets considerable weightage in the selection of candidates and vote-casting during elections. With India declaring itself a welfare state, formal accountability of public servants has increased manifold compared to what it was during the colonial days of India.

The above scenario keeps on undergoing a continuous

process of change. Therefore, the outlook of the people and their values are bound to change so as to adjust to the realities of the new situations created by science, technology, political and other factors.

Defining Value-System:

Value-system is the fusion of moral and spiritual values. The Report on the Religious and Moral Education, prepared by the Committee headed by Shri Sri Prakash defined moral behaviour as 'the conduct of man towards man in various situations in which human beings come together in home, social and economic fields and in the life of outside world generally. —Anything that helps us to behave properly towards others is of moral value.[8]

Spiritual values are also moral values; but in this case there is emphasis on the inner-self of the individual and his relation with the Supreme Being. Anything that takes the individual out of one-self and inspires one to sacrifice for a great cause of for the good of others is spiritual.

It may be conceded here that there is no universally accepted definition of 'good' or 'bad'. As pointed out earlier, these terms are related to time, place and persons.Good may, by some persons, be equated with the will of God and evil as an inducement of Satan. Good is also identified with pleasure and evil with suffering. There is hardly any defined frontier between licit and illicit. Such a definition is only possible on the basis of certain socially accepted norms or governmental laws. It is easier to discriminate the lawful from the unlawful.

Morality is concerned, both, with beliefs and actions which are in conformity with the social norms shaped, modified and chiselled over a length of time. In ancient Greece, there was emphasis on 'beliefs' whereas in ancient India, the stress was on 'action'. However, action had to be in conformity with Dharma. Thus action itself had moral spiritual base. Manu, the great Indian codifier, on the strength of the Vedas and the Smritis, says that doing noble actions is the highest duty (dharma) of man.

"आचारः परमो धर्मः श्रत्युक्त स्मार्त एव च"[9]

The belief about what is right and what is wrong; what ought to be done and what ought not to be done is generally defined as moral belief. It is a matter of common observance that the beliefs of the people in any group are not always in consonance with their actions. The fact that adultery may be regarded immoral by many people in a country, yet some people may by involved in this practice and no law may exist against adultery in the country, can be cited as an example in this regard. Numerous religious customs may not stand the test of a rational debate, yet many people believe in them and adhere to them. One cannot categorise such beliefs as 'right beliefs'. There is, therefore, an inherent problem in identifying 'right beliefs', and 'right actions'.

Further, sometimes an action may appear to be moral, yet it may not be so. Reduction in prices of consumer goods would be moral if it is intended to help the poor and the general public but not so if its motive is to boost up the sales. Therefore, the 'will' and the 'motive' behind the action is very important. An act becomes moral only if the doer acts in a 'desirable way' of his own free-will for the good of others.

At times, an act may not be in consonance with the social mores, yet it may not be immoral. For example, the wide-spread students demonstrations and marches in Beijing (capital of China) spread over several days in May, 1989 and in violation of the martial law imposed by the Chinese Government could not be termed immoral, because basically the slogan of the students was "We want Mr. Science and Mr. Democracy" :

Therefore, notwithstanding the fact that it is difficult to precisely define the philosophical and abstract concept 'morality' one may attempt to understand this term in the following ways.

(a) The basis of morality is right belief and right action.
(b) The element of free-will of the doer is fundamental to any moral act. The doer must adhere to the moral act inspite of a temptation to deviate from it.
(c) Moral act extends both over physiological and psychological domains.

Classification of Values :

(i) Moral and spiritual values may be classified in several ways. In terms of importance, values may be divided into the following three groups.

(a) Trivial values, such as the type of clothes one should wear while going to a restaurant. Today, even the dress that one wears at a funeral or while attending a marriage party has come to occupy a trivial significance, particularly in the urban context.
(b) More substantial beliefs, such as the ones which also effect people other than the belief-holder himself. These include punctuality, cleanliness, etc. etc.
(c) Fundamental or perennial and emphemeral beliefs, such as practice of truthfulness, spirit of patriotism, kindness towards all life etc. etc.

(ii) The great Indian sage Vatsyayana relates virtues and vices to human faculties and gives the following classification.[10]

(a) Virtues of body : charity, helping the needy, social service.
(b) Virtues of speech: truthfulness, benevolence, gentleness, recitation of scriptures.
(c) Virtues of mind: kindness, unworldliness, piety.
(d) Vices of body: cruelty, theft, sexual indulgence.
(e) Vices of speech: falsehood, harshness, scandal.
(f) Vices of mind: hatred, covetousness, disbelief.

(iii) In terms of social order, values may be classified as political, economic, social, cultural, spiritual, aesthetic and individual values. Thus values encompass the entire gamut of life. According to the Indian philosophy, individual interest may be sacrificed for that of the family, the interest of the family for that of the clan and all interests for that of the soul. According to Indian spiritual philosophers, individual soul is a part and parcel of the universal soul.

(iv) There has been no time in the history of man, when he had no moral values. The values, therefore, can also be grouped as ancient, medieval and modern values. Some people hold that there is nothing modern in the value-system of the present age. For example, according to them the so-called modern concept of egalitarianism existed in olden days in the form of tolerance; and scientific temper in the shape of indepth analysis of the phenomenon of life and forces of nature. It may be relevant to point out here that when under pressure coal gets transformed into diamond, it is not called coal. It is given a new name, which everyone accepts. The same argument can be applicable in case of ancient and modern values also.

Origin and Evolution of Moral Values :

All morality, according to one belief, is deemed to have originated from God, His son, His Messengers and His Avtars. Revealed scriptures and great works are other important sources of dissemination of moral values. It is believed that the sun god presented code of laws to Hammurabi; God gave commandments to Moses; Zeus gave moral sense to humans so that they could cooperate with each other and match the beasts who are stronger and speedier than man. Myths such as the one relating to the dual between the gods and the demons (virtue and vice), where gods are shown victorious in the end help in promoting moral values among the people. These may be lies but they are 'noble lies' which originate and disseminate moral values.

Genetic affinity is considered to be an important factor in parental altruism.

Anthropologists and historians believe that when homo sapiens started living in families, its members developed a sense of obligation to each other.

Man may have, as well, imbibed moral behaviour from his animal ancestors. Many animals abide by the norms of mutual cooperation and help. Strikingly, wolves bring the meat of the kill to the members of their group who are not present at the kill; dolphins support their sick to come up to the water surface and breathe. The famous story of the persevering spider which inspired the disappointed king Robert Bruce, to fight once again is included in the school text-books to instil this quality of the spider among students.

The ancient seers of India, perhaps, gave a very highly rational explanation in this context when they said that cosmic order (rta) was the foundation of human ethics. They felt that the beauty in earth, sky and nature, as a whole, emerged from this cosmic law (rta). "Gradually, the cosmic sense of rta as Natural Law developed into the social sense of rta as Moral Law". In other words, morality was as essential to bring about beauty and harmony in life as the cosmic order in nature. Punishment is not based on whims; but it is the result of wrong actions only. One could enjoy life if one could ensure order in one's activities. Rta, in a way, was the basis of the ancient Indian moral laws.

Great men, or for that matter any group of dominant persons, greatly influence the value-system of the society. The Bhaktas and the Sufis, during the medieval period of Indian history, inspired people towards chastity, renunciation, desirelessness and other similar values. Material aspirations came to be looked upon as undivine. The feudal system and dynastic rules of this age, whipped up sex urge among some classes of people and also produced a class of flatterers and courtiers. In the modern era, Raja Ram Mohan Roy, Swami Vivekananda, Sir Syed Ahmed Khan, Bedrudin Tyabji, Madan Mohan Malviya, Lala Lajpat Rai, Swami Dayanand Saraswati, Mahatama Gandhi (1869-1948) and a galaxy of other reformers worked for the independence of the country, better deal for women, social justice for the backward classes and many other values which are enshrined in the Indian Constitution.

The Constitution of India, with its 64 amendments (till 1989), is an important source of the present-day Indian value-system. It lists ten Fundamental Duties for each citizen.[11] The Preamble of the Constitution emphasises certain important values. These may be called national values. Cessation of cold war between countries may be categorised as an international value. Preservation of environment is a national as well as an international value.

The governments try to uphold and promote these values through laws, penal codes and other measures.

Parmatha Nath Bose divides the evolution of human values chronologically in three stages.[12]

(a) During the early stages, the predatory man, like animals, sought comfort in material and emotional gratification. Emotional expression in humans found expression through arts, such as poetry, painting, sculpture etc. Thus this is the first level of achievement of the value-system in human society.

(b) During the intermediate stage, intellectual development separates him from the animals. He begins to examine physical and psychical processes. It is at this juncture that science and philosophy are born and scientific and philosophical values take shape.

(c) At the advanced stage of his development, man's spiritual faculty has developed and he begins to seek happiness from within rather than from without. Two faculties develop at this stage:

- (i) spiritual which inspires belief in supernatural beings; and
- (ii) moral faculty which enables a person to perceive moral good or evil independent of expediency, consideration of utility or physical welfare or suffering.

Incidentally this analysis would give students of ethics some idea about the level of cultural heights that India had attained thousands of years ago with her highly developed spiritual culture which remains, even today, unrivalled in the world.

Essentials of Morality:

All human values are shaped by our wants. Man has material as well as spiritual wants. These may be termed as wants of the outer and inner life respectively. The former promote qualities of industry, order, perseverence etc., which have a survival value. The wants of inner life promote cultural values like humility, mercy, self-sacrifice etc. Neither of these wants should be considered inferior to the other.

A moral code would have a greater appeal for the people in general if it is simple and not complicated. The Buddhism was able to make a mass appeal because its teachings were simple as compared to Brahmanism which in the days of Buddha had become highly complicated. No moral code would be acceptable in the modern scientific age unless it has a rational basis and can appeal to one's reason.

Socrates, the great Greek philosopher, emphasised right knowledge as the true basis for moral actions. Goethe, on the other hand, observed that man comes to know himself not through reflection but through action or conduct only. He said, "Do thy duty and thou wilt know what thou art".[13] According to the ancient Indian thought it is the conduct (Aacharan) which determines the moral standards of an individual or a group. It is said you are judged not by what you say; but what you are in totality.

Importance of Value-Education :

Is the primary aim of moral education to have more scientists, better cricketers, large number of tennis-stars or athletes who can win more gold medals for the country? Perhaps, not. The chief aim of value education is to achieve maximum human resource development so as to improve our total life. One can not do better than to quote here Edwin Markhani in order to bring out the great importance of value-education. He said :

> "We are blind until we see that in the human plan, nothing is worth the making if it does not make the man. Why build these cities glorious if man unbuilded goes? In vain we build the world, unless the builder also grows".

References and Notes

1. Myers, Philip VANN NESS: *History As Past Ethics - An Introduction to the History of Morals*: Boston: GINN and Company,1913.
2. Hob house : *Morals in Evolution*, Vol (1), 1906; p. 307; (quoted in Myers History As Past Ethics; p.296).
3. Myers *History As Past Ethics;* p. 180.
4. *Ibid;* p.62.
5. Read Murtada Mutahhari,*The Rights of Women in Islam*, Translated by World Organisation for Islamic Studies, Tehran (Iran), 1981.
6. Surendra Kumar; *Vishudha Manusmriti;* Arsh Sahitya Prachar Trust, Delhi; 1986, 91-93/(66-68) p. 319.
7. Mayers *History As Past Ethics.* p. 52
8. *Report of the Committee on Religious and Moral Instruction*, Union Ministry of Education, New Delhi, 1959,para 30.
9. *Vishudha Manusmriti;* 108/55; p.62.
10. S. Cromwell Crawford; *The Evolution of Hindu Ethical Ideals;*

Asian Studies Program, University of Hawaii; The University Press of Hawaii; 1982; p. 147.

11. *The Constitution of India*; Government of India, Ministry of Law, Justice and Company Affairs; Article 51A.

12. Bose, Parmatha Nath; *Epochs of Civilisation*; Asian Educational Service, New Delhi; p. 339.

13. *Beyond the Punitive Society Operant Conditions*, Social and Political Aspects, ed. by Harvey Wheeler; Pub. W.H. Freeman and Company, San Francisco; 1973, p. 199.

2

Decline in Values

There is hardly any issue on which one may find complete unanimity of views in the society. The situation is no different in the case of the value- system. Many people feel that there is, at present, a state of total chaos in the society so far as moral values are concerned. However, a number of people do not share deep concern over the so-called deterioration of moral values. The great scientist Darwin had remarked that mankind is continuously progressing on a course of evolution. Undoubtedly, he must have been alluding to the biological factors only. The great spiritual leader Aurobindo Ghosh had said that the homo sapien would steadily attain super-manhood and that there is no returning for him to the lower forms of life. Some people hold that the psychological man has, in modern times, been left much behind the physiological man and the cultural march of human race has failed to match its technological progress. On the contrary, there is a class of people who feel that from the predatory man to the present-day civilised homo sapien, man's cultural advancement excels his achievement in any other field.

The data collected for the study indicated a convergence of views. Bulk of respondents feel that there has been a decline in moral values. To the statement that "over the past 5-10 years, moral values among Indians have declined", (G-I), the 881 respondents expressed their opinions as follows.*

---

* Note :(i) Figures in brackets below the columns c to f indicate percentages, whereas such figures below column b give the number of respondents in the corresponding category.

(ii) Though this kind of analysis was done in the case of several categories of respondents, but the entire bunch of statistics has not been given here in order to avoid confusion.

(iii) The above system has been followed all through in this work.

Decline of Moral Values

a	b	c	d	e	f
S.No.	Category	Number Agreeing	No. undecided	No. disagreed	No. of persons who expressed no opinion
(1)	Total no. of Respondents (881)	775	61	44	1
(2)	Respondents in the age-group 25-40 years (233)	208 (89.3)	10 (4.3)	15 (6.4)	— (0)
(3)	Respondents above 40 years of age (573)	507 (88.5)	39 (6.8)	26 (4.5)	1 (0.2)
(4)	High School or equivalent (98)	84 (85.7)	6 (6.1)	8 (8.2)	— (0)
(5)	MA and above or equivalent (405)	359 (88.6)	27 (6.7)	18 (4.4)	1 (0.3)
(6)	Educationists (21)	21 (95.5)	0 (0)	1 (4.5)	0 (0)
(7)	Advocates (10)	7 (70)	1 (10)	2 (20)	0 (0)

Of the total 881 non-student general category respondents,88 per cent concurred with the above (G-1)** statement, 5 per cent of them expressed their disagreement to it and the remaining 7 per cent were undecided on this issue. The moral crisis has, perhaps, became so obvious that the level of education did not make any significant difference in their view-point on this statement. The highest degree of agreement was expressed by the educationists and the least by the advocates. Reasons for this are, perhaps, obvious! Even in the case of the latter, there is a high degree of agreement about the decline in moral values.

** 'G' refers to the questionnaire meant for the general public, other than students. In the questionnaire meant for students the abbreviation used is 's'. Numbers 1,2,3,——18 indicate the serial order of the statement in the corresponding questionnaire. Thus G-I would stand for statement 1 in the questionaire meant for respondents in the general category.

Perhaps people of every generation always feel that the values have declined in their time as compared to what they were in the 'golden past'. Even when the Greek civilization had reached its heights, Plato (427-347 B.C.) stated more than two millennia ago;

"What is happening to our young people. They disrespect their elders, they disobey their parents. They ignore the laws. They riot in the street, inflamed with wild notions. Their morals are decaying. What is to become of them?"

There may be valid reasons to lament over the loss of values in a society; but sometimes it may be difficult to pin-point whether a value-system is undergoing a metamor-phosis or whether it is declining. For example, during the Indian freedom struggle of 1930's and 40s, many young men and women left their studies, jobs and families to work for their country against the colonial rule. Many in the older generation had then opposed the action of the youths; but later on it was these youths that were acclaimed as national heroes. In 1967, when the students of the Wisconsin University (U.S.A.) staged a massive demonstration against the napalming of North Vietnam by America, they did not receive the requisite general public support in their struggle; but subsequent events proved that the young students were right.

According to the Rishis of ancient India, gods and demons; creation and destruction; good and evil are the products of the same Cosmic Energy. They have coexisted from the inception of this universe. No Age or society ever had good without evil or evil without good and decline in moral values only means absence of a proper balance between the two. It is the domination of demonic destructive, evil and such like tendencies over the godly, constructive and noble tendencies which amounts to the decline in values.

Moral values have an ideological and a philosophical basis. It would not be wrong to say that during the feudal as well as colonial past, these bases were greatly weakened. The struggle for country's independence did, to some extent, restore the ideological basis, but within a couple of decades after independence the hand of the clock again started reversing. Today, we are at a stage where it is difficult to state categorically if any organised section of the society is seriously and consistently working for upholding moral values.

Causes for the Decline of Values

There are various causes for the decline of values in a society. One can concede that the fall in the Indian value-system is a part of world-wide apathy to moral values.

Further, moral values are generally nourished by the middle class. The rich are generally indifferent to the value-system of the society; and the poor, because of inherent economic and other constraints cannot live up to it. Today, the aspirations of the neo-middle class have increased greatly and the value-system has been subordinated to these aspirations. This has subscribed to the lowering of moral values.

Science and material progress has also greatly contributed to the fall of social and spiritual values. Science has led to industrialisation; industrialisation to capitalism; capitalism to over-production and concentration of wealth in the hands of the few; and all this to the political and economic exploitation of the many by a few.

The statement contained in the questionnaire in regard to the causes of the fall of moral values in the society read as follows :

The following are the causes for the fall in values in the society:–

(a) Absence of proper religious teaching.
(b) Fall in moral values of our political leaders.
(c) Mass media adopting no proper policy to build moral standards in the society. (G-16)

The scores for these statements are given below :

Grading Causes of Moral Decline

Statement	Number of persons who allotted first, second or third positions to the statement.			Number of persons who left the statement blank.	Weighted score*
	I position	II position	III position		
(a)	224	233	301	123	54.5%
(b)	328	260	170	123	63.3%
(c)	212	269	277	123	54.9%

* Weighted scores in such cases were calculated as follows: For the I, II and III positions, the scores allotted were 3,2 and 1 respectively. No score was allotted where the statement was left blank without any reaction. To illustrate, the score for statement at (a) above was calculated as below :

$$\frac{(224 \times 3) + (233 \times 2) + (301 \times 1)}{881 \times 3} \times \frac{100}{1} = 54.5\%$$

Thus among the reasons which were given in the questionnaire, the fall in moral values of our political leaders was considered by the respondents to have contributed significantly to a greater extent than the other two values to the decline of values in the society. It confirms the view-point held by many people that the value-system emerges from the seat of power. Absence of proper religious teaching was given the third place in this regard. Nearly 14 per cent of the respondents did not express any opinion on this statement.

In this respect, Caudwell says, "And the unparalleled increase in the productive power has given birth, not to peace, plenty, and happiness, but to war, famine and misery. Anarchy is the keynote of crisis in all spheres. ....Why then have not all the psycho-analysis, Eddingtons, Keynes, Spengiers, and bishops who have surveyed the scene, been able to locate a source of infection common to all modern cultures. For answer, these people must take to themselves, the words of Herzen: 'We are not the doctors, we are the disease.[1]

Assessing Leadership on Value-Scale

Leadership in all fields tends to influence the value-system of the common man also. This hypothesis is truer when viewed in the context of the politicians, the teachers and the parents. The impact of the politicians,is on a wide cross-section of the society, whereas the impact of the teachers and parents is deeper on the childern as among other things, it starts working during the early and impressionable years of the individuals. Therefore, an attempt was made through the questionnaire meant for the general public and the one meant for the students to rate politicians,teachers and parents on the basis of some of the statements that follows.

Politicians:

"Keeping in view the conduct of majority of Indian political leaders, one concludes that their quality is —

(a) Of the desired level

or

(b) Average

or

(c) Below the desired level." (G-8)

Of the 881 respondents in the G group*, 848 i.e., 96.2 per cent opted for one of the above three options. 3 per cent were undecided

* Respondents in the (non-student) general public category.

and the remaining 0.8 per cent recorded disagreement to these options.

Rating the Politicians

Option	Number of Persons Agreeing	
(a)	45	(5.%)
(b)	154	(17.5%)
(c)	649	(73.6%)
Total (881)	848	(96.2%)

The general public have given a clear verdict that the majority of the Indian political leaders are below the desired level.

In this context, one should not forget that the class of politicians during and immediately after the country's independence struggle were highly respected by the public. Leaders like Mahatama Gandhi, Jawahar Lal Nehru, Sardar Patel, Rafi Ahmad Kidwai, Khan Abdul Ghaffar Khan, are revered even today. They made great sacrifices for the national good. The profiles of the politicians who made up the country's Constituent Assembly also fall in the same category. However, while talking of the majority of the present-day politicians, the picture draws a blank.

The Bofors, and the Oil and Natural Gas Commission deals bring a lot of disrepute to the politicians.[2]

No doubt, the charges of nepotism, accumulation of undeclared black-money etc. are not confined to the politicians alone, but this does not exonerate the politicians from being responsible for malpractices and setting an unworthy example of leadership before their people.

Commenting on the criminalisation of politics with muscle and money power and multitude of corrupt practices,one of the English dailies of national standing had once remarked as follows:

" Every passing day reveals disturbing evidence of growing criminalisation of Indian politics. The results of Sunday's (16.10.88) elections for the pramukhs (chiefs) of block development committees in U.P are the latest manifestations. In several districts in east U.P criminals or candidates supported by them, won elections convincingly at the expense of the candidates backed by political parties. Most remarkable was the victory of a known bandit chief of Banda district. Not only did he win, four of his candidates also won. A well-known mafia don won, unopposed, from Sitapur block, which is right next to Lucknow— the State Capital. All this should come as no surprise. The link between criminals and politicians has assumed alarming proportions in the Hindi belt since 1967, when booth-capturing first occurred on a massive scale in Bihar. —But this phenomenon is not confined to the Congress; the links between Janta big-wigs and mafia dons of Dhanbad are not even sought to be covert."[3]

The following remark by a scholar- poet-politician, a former Minister in the country's Union Cabinet, and later an Ambassador, is highly significant.

" Of course the present-day politician is rated differently from the luminaries of the freedom struggle; but then he is only elected by the people. Perhaps, no people can rise much above their moral and cultural ethos in elections also."

Teachers:

Statement S-10 read as follows: *

(i) "Keeping in view the conduct of majority of Indian teachers, one concludes that their quality is—

(a) Of the desired level

OR

(b) Average

OR

(c) Below the desired level." (S–10)

(ii) "The following factors are responsible for lowering the status of teachers :

(a) Lack of scholarship in teachers;
(b) Teachers' lust for money;
(c) Absence of sacrifice among teachers for their students."

In the second statement, the respondents were asked to grade the various reasons in descending order of importance. (S–14)*

The guru or the acharya, as the teacher was known in this country in ancient times, had a place of reverence in India. He was the repository of knowledge and a person of exemplary high character. During the period of education of the student, the guru assumed the responsibility of acting as the parent of his students and the students were part and parcel of his family. The mother

* 'S' refer to the questionnaire for students and the number 14, for that matter any number in its place, refers to the serial number of the statement in this questionnaire.

and the father gave physical birth to the child; and the teacher gave the second, i.e. the intellectual birth to him. Being a religious as well as an intellectual leader of the society, the teacher enjoyed great respect, even in the court of the kings. The Indian teacher basked in the sunshine of this glory (though somewhat to a lesser degree with the passage of time) till the advent of the British rule. During the British rule, education became procurable and saleable for money. Its past sanctity started vanishing. Any assessment of the present day Indian teachers, must obviously take the above historical background into account. However, the Indian ethos demand a certain level of accomplishment from the teachers. Once they enter the teaching profession, they must come up to the expectations of the society. In order to come up to the expected level of accomplishment, the teachers need to have some idea of their image which they now have in the public eyes.

Rating the Teachers

Option	Number of Persons Agreeing	Percentage
Quality of teacher is–		
(a) Of the desired level OR	32	12
(b) Average OR	182	68.2
(c) Below the desired level.	46	17.2
Total	261	97.4%

Six, i.e. 2.2 per cent respondents were undecided and one (0.4%) of the school students (male) expressed disagreement with the statement that the teacher's quality was below the desired level. Thus, by and large, teachers have been rated as mediocres by the students. Students' rating of teachers may give teachers some pseudo-satisfaction when compared with the following assessment of the politicians by the general public.

Comparative Assessment of the Quality of

OPTION	Politicians	Teachers
(a) Of the desired level OR	5.1 p.c.	12.0 p.c.
(b) Average OR	17.5 p.c.	68.2 p.c.
(c) Below the desired level	73.6 p.c.	17.2 p.c.

It goes without saying that the academic and behavioural excellence of teachers will tend to make their students also likewise. Similarly, the mediocrity of teachers is likely to produce the products of an average quality only.

Teachers have, thus, to accept their share of the existing social malaise, especially in respect of their students. It has been aptly remarked, "Teachers can escape from their influence over the moral and spiritual development of their pupils by closing their schools."[4] Teachers are charged with an important responsibility of guiding their students. By entering the teaching profession they, ipso-facto, accept this responsibility. In order to fulfil this obligation, they must raise their own level of conduct in their own eyes as well as in the estimation of the public. The Urdu poet was not wrong when he said—

"Rahbar-e-gum gashta ko lazim hai apni ahtiat,
Rah pe lane se pahle rah pe ana bhi hai."

'A guide has to be very careful about himself. He has to be on the right track himself, before he can bring others onto it.'

It would be appropriate to diagnose here a couple of causes responsible for lowering the status of teachers.

Grading Causes Responsible for Lowering Teachers' Status

Statement	Number of persons who alloted first, second or third positions to this statement			Number of persons who left the statement blank	Weighted score
	I	II	III		
(a)	42	80	142	3	53.4%
(b)	116	82	66	3	72.1%
(c)	106	102	55	4	72%

Thus in the opinion of the college as well school students it is not so much the lack of scholarship as the other two factors which are responsible for bringing down the status of teachers. Their lust for money and absence of the element of sacrifice among teachers have been considered almost equally important factors for lowering the status of teachers. In this regard a respondent (a colonel in the Defence Services) had remarked very appropriately: "The ethos of the teachers needs to change from those of the merchants to those of the gurus."

Parents:

In this connection, the students were to react to the following statement.

"Yonger generation will show more respect to their parents, if

(a) Parents give greater freedom to their children as children grow in age;

(b) Parents spend more time with their children;

(c) Parents themselves keep adjusting to changing social values". (S-15)

Students were required to rank the above statements.

Parents Assessed By Children

Statement	Overall score as given by all student-respondents.	Scores given by male students in		Scores given by female students in	
		schools	colleges	schools	colleges
(a)	45.8%	46.6%	51%	42.6%	44.3%
(b)	66.9%	64.8%	66.6%	69.4%	68.1%
(c)	83.1%	88.6%	79.4%	88%	81%

It is interesting to observe that the order assigned to various statements by the total group and different sub-groups of students is identical.

All students, whether in schools or colleges, also want their parents to spend more time with them, for this greatly contributes to establishing emotional rapport between the parents and their children. Such a rapport is necessary so as to ward off psychological problems among children. In some cases where the parents are educated, dialogues and meetings between parents and children are also a source of education for the latter.

However, these meetings can be fruitful only if parents with the changing times keep on adjusting to the changing social values.

Present day parents are not what their parents were and their children cannot be what they are. This is a fast changing world where scientific discoveries, mass-media, and international influences are revolutionising the thought-processes which were so far circumscribed when these factors were absent or had a limited impact. In case where the parents refuse to adjust to the transforming social values, the rift between parents and their children is bound to ensue sooner than later. It is worth noting that the young students have not accorded high priority to have greater freedom.

It is difficult to say that the moral values have totally declined. For every teacherous traitor, there has always been a courageous fighter in the world. If there are terrorists, there are Vinoba's and Mother Teresa's also to heal the wounds of the oppressed. Of course, the cases of moral decline are sensationally highlighted through the mass media whereas hundreds of people leading a pious life do not catch the attention of the mass media because they do not create sensation. Notwithstanding all this, a fairly large section of the society feels that the moral values in the present-day Indian society have declined. Other important causes, besides the ones stated above, for the fall in the value-system, may be summed up as follows.

(i) The gap between the material and the spiritual progress is an important cause of the present moral crisis. Nuclear capability is a great (material) achievement, but our failure to coordinate it with moral values poses serious dangers to the human race. We have, somehow, forgotten that there is a psychological man behind the physical man. Stating this idea philosophically, the ancient Indian had declared that the cosmic matter (prakriti) coupled with cosmic spirit (pursha) alone gives meaning to life. The import of this great thought seems to have been lost somewhere.

(ii) The fall in values in modern times is attributable to over-emphasis on wealth power, and consumerism.

(iii) The present social milieu, as some people believe, is such that it takes us to the moral downfall. While criticising the social environs, we should remember that the individual is a block as well as a builder of the social system. The social ethos depend on the ethos of the individuals constituting the group, therefore, why not to start the process of moral regeneration of the society with ourselves?

(iv) When India became free, the West was highly affluent and was immersed in the consumer-goods civilisation.

It had a glamour for every developing country. Indians also wanted to reach the same stage of affluence. The short-cut approach to it lay through the sacrifice of values. Our weak spiritual and educational background, which was the result of the colonial rule, contributed to our undermining the higher values of life.

(v) Western literature introduced some new trends in the Indian literature, some of which were unhealthy. These trends brimmed with sex, crime and violence. This had an adverse impact on the social ethos. What is true of literature, is true of films also, which is literature on a silvery-screen.

(vi) There has been a sea-change in the political, economic and social structure of the human society during the last about 150 years. Princely states have given way to democratic systems. Altruism has been replaced by self-centredness, acquisition and consumerism. Galloping urbanisation has ushered in the apartment-culture and pushed off the rural life values, including socialisation. With the ever-increasing speed in life and both the parents racing from one appointment to another, there is limited socialisation even at home. All this has brought about changs in our outlook to the existing value-system. The trend needs to be rectified.

(vii) Democracy has made a great contribution to alleviating the lot of the common man, particularly the down-trodden and the backward. However, one cannot be oblivious to its negative role in regard to nurturing of higher moral values. Winston Churchil once described democracy as the worst form of government till a better alternative was available. Pramatha Bose said :

> "There is, perhaps, no tyranny more incompatible with higher culture than the tyranny of an ignorant democracy. —The leaders of Greek thought, from Pythagoras to Aristotle, were mostly persecuted, some of them sent into exile and some condemned to death."[5]

In a democracy, the lower strata are elevated at the expense of the higher strata. Under democratic process the influence of the 'higher strata', spheres of art, literature etc. included, gets weakened. Knowledge extends over wider surface but loses in depth. Authors have to adapt to the capabilities of the 'common' man. There is trend towards writing light rather than thoughtful literature.

All this highlights the need for an enlightened and a fresh approach to the important question of value-education.

References and Notes

1. Candwell, Christopher; *Studies and Further Studies in a Dying Culture*, Review Press, New York, London,1971; p.xix.

2. (i) Bofors Deal : It was a 1700 crore rupees deal with Sweden for the purchase of 155 mm Bofor field-guns. It was alleged by some political parties in the opposition in the Parliament that there was a pay-off to the tune of about 64 crore rupees (in Swedish currency) in this deal. A Joint Parliamentary Committee of the two Houses of Parliament probed into the matter; but it could not identify the agency which had been paid 64 crore rupees.

   (ii) Indian Oil and Natural Gas Commision Deal : It was alleged that for a 100 crore rupees order for pipelines placed on the Sumitomo Corporation of Japan by the Indian Oil and Natural Gas Commission (ONGC), an Indian intermediary who was cut into the deal in 1983, received 6.61 crore rupees. The money is alleged to have been originally deposited in London bank and later brought to India sometime by 1986-87.

3. The Times of India, New Delhi, October 22, 1988, editorial column.

4. Downey Meriel; *Moral Education : Theory and Practice*, Harper and Row, London; p.1.

5. Bose, Pramatha Nath; *Epochs of Civilisation*; Asian Educational Services, New Delhi; pp.50-51.

3

Need for Value-Education

An important feature of value-education is the ability of the educator and the educand to discriminate between right and wrong. What may be nectar for one may be poison for another. We may be clearing forests to build human habitats, which is a laudable objective, but in the process we may be depriving animals of their natural shelter and foou and humanity of many environmental benefits. In many Indian communities, a wedlock between a girl and a boy may not be permissible unless the two are removed from each other by a gap of some generations; whereas among some, marriage between cousins may be auspicious. A debate on the subject can go *ad infinitum* without coming to any precise conclusion; but as pointed out earlier every community has its own written as well as unwritten behavioural norms which it expects its members to observe.

In order to decide if the educational institutions should play some part in the dissemination of these accepted norms, the following statement was included in the questionnaire for students.

"Value-education i.e., education regarding discrimination between what is right or wrong, should be imparted in schools and colleges." (S-1)

The reaction of the five categories of students, constituting the total student-population of 267 was as follows.

Educational Institutions to Impart Value-Education

a S.No.	b Category.	c Number Agreeing.	d Number Undecided.	e Number Disagreed.	f Number of persons who expressed no opinion.
(1)	Total no. of student respondents (267)	254 (95.2)	6 (2.2)	6 (2.2)	1 (0.4)
(2)	School students (Male) (70)	68 (97.2)	1 (1.4)	1 (1.4)	- -
(3)	School Students (Female) (86)	84 (97.6)	1 (1.2)	1 (1.2)	- -
(4)	College Students (M)* (34)	27 (79.6)	4 (11.8)	3 (8.8)	- -
(5)	African College students (M)* studying in the Delhi Colleges. (7)	7 (100)	3 -	4 -	- -
(6)	Indian College students (F)* (70)	68 (97.2)	- -	1 (1.4)	1 (1.4)

It is thus observed that the every category of students expressed high degree of agreement for making a provision of value-education in the educational institutions.** Speaking in comparative terms, more of college students (males) expressed

* (i) Abbreviations M and F stand for Male and Female respectively throughout this work.

** (ii) The following norm has been adopted in this study for categorisation of scores :

Below 26% Poor | 50% Average | 51-74% Above Average

26-49% Below Average | Above 74% High

their disagreement with the statement or were undecided in this regard.

Therefore, if one were to work for a programme of moral or value-education in our educational institutions, one is likely to come across a receptive rather than an indifferent audience, provided the programme is given due importance in the curricula and the teacher imparting value-education is capable of doing justice to the job.

The following news-item appearing in one of the national dailies in India shows that there is a world-wide demand for imparting moral education to the students.

"The (U.K.) Government is to direct its latest attack on violence, disorder and crime at children as young as seven". In a Cabinet meeting it was felt that 'the roots of criminality' must be tackled early and that "moral dimension will be added to the new national curriculm".

Sometime earlier to it in the economic summit in Toronto (Canada), Mrs. Thatcher, the British Prime Minister had raised her concern on the behavioural problems of the young people. She said that although western nations had gone a long way to bring about a technological change, they had to do much in terms of training people to have respect for the law. The Government (of U.K.) had proposed preparing experimental lessons for the youth with this objective in view. For example, in such lessons the school going youth may be told about a young man who drinks, steals a car, becomes a hit-and-run driver and ultimately one day lands in the custody of the police. The lesson may depict the consequence (jail etc.) to be faced by the delinquent youth, misery of the family whose members had been hit by this criminal and also the misery of the criminal's own family because of his unlawful act. For this purpose parents, teachers and media have to unite. Teachers cannot provide lessons which are the responsibility of the parents.[1]

Resembling the above statement (S-1) in the questionnaire for students, there was a statement (G-13) in the questionnaire for the general public. The statement was as follows:

" Moral education *i.e.*, education regarding what is right or wrong should be imparted-

a) In schools
b) In colleges
c) Through mass media such as radio, TV, newspapers etc. (G-13)

Number of persons who agreed, disagreed with the above three parts of the statement or were un-decided in this regard was as follows :

Media For Imparting Moral Education

a	b	c	d	e	f
S.No.	Category	No. Agree-ing.	No. Un-decided.	No. Dis-agreeing.	No. of persons who expressed no opinion
(a) In schools	Total no. of respondents (881)	717 (81.6)	136 (15.5)	16 (1.8)	10 (1.1)
(b) In colleges	Total no. of respon-dents (881)	510 (57.9)	315 (35.8)	43 (4.9)	13 (1.4)
(c) Through mass media	-do-	655 (74.4)	194 (22)	16 (1.8)	16 (1.8)

The above statistics show that the elements of disagreement and indecision are comparatively higher in the case of part (b) of the statement. Also the largest number of the respondents appeared to be of the opinion that moral education should be imparted in schools.

Parts (a), (b) and (c) of the statement were further analysed with reference to age, educational qualifications and income of the respondents. Some of the results obtained were as follows:

Statement 13 (a) **Analysis with Reference to Ages of the Respondents**

a	b	c	d	e	f
S.No.	Category of Respondents	No. Agreeing	No. Un-decided	No. Dis-agreeing	No. of persons who expressed no opinion.
1.	Below 18 years (11)	9 (81.9)	2 (18.2)	-	-

a	b	c	d	e	f
2.	18-25 years (52)	37 (71.2)	15 (28.8)	- -	- -
3.	25-40 years (234)	191 (81.6)	38 (16.2)	2 (0.9)	3 (1.3)
4.	Above 40 years (574)	474 (82.6)	79 (13.8)	14 (2.4)	7 (1.2)
5.	Those who did not indicate their ages (10)	8 (80)	2 (20)	-	-

Statement 13 (b) **Analysis with Reference to Educational Qualifications of the Respondents**

S.No.	Category. of Respondents	Number Agreeing.	Number Undecided.	Number Disagreeing.	Number of persons who expressed no opinion.
a	b	c	d	e	f
(1)	Below High school (15)	6 (40)	7 (46.7)	2 (13.3)	- -
(2)	High school or equivalent (123)	66 (53.7)	50 (40.6)	5 (4.1)	2 (1.6)
(3)	B.A. or equivalent (267)	157 (58.8)	96 (35.9)	13 (4.9)	1 (0.4)
(4)	M.A. or above or equivalent (464)	274 (59.0)	157 (33.8)	23 (5)	10 (2.2)
(5)	Those did not indicate their educational qualifications (12)	7 (58.3)	5 (41.7)	- -	- -

Statement 13 (c)		Analysis with Reference to Monthly Income of the Respondents			
a	b	c	d	e	f
(1)	Below Rs. 1000	16	11	-	1
	(28)	(57.1)	(39.3)	-	(3.6)
(2)	Rs.1000-1999	68	27	1	2
	(98)	(69.4)	(27.5)	(1)	(2)
(3)	Rs. 2000-3999	246	75	10	3
	(334)	(73.6)	(22.5)	(3)	(0.9)
(4)	Rs. 4000 or above	318	74	5	10
	(407)	(78.1)	(18.2)	(1.2)	(2.5)
(5)	Those who did not indicate their		7	7	- -
	income	7	7		
	(14)	(50)	(50)	-	-

The analysis in the case of the statement 13(a) indicates that in comparison to the remaining age-groups of the respondents, those between 18-25 years of age expressed lesser degree of agreement (of 71.2%) with this statement. The remaining 28.8% of the respondents in this group were undecided.

Analysis of the reactions of the respondents on the basis of their educational qualifications revealed that quite a large number of respondents in every group, sub-group seemed to be undecided on the issue whether of moral education programme should be introduced at the college stage. The reasons for this could be as follows :

(a) Higher education is a stage of specialisation in one or the other discipline, therefore general education in morals was not supported by any sub-group as was done in the case of the school stage.

(b) The college students are mature enough to decide for themselves as to what is right and what is wrong.

It would be interesting here to study the attitude of male and female college teachers to the same statement *i.e.* 13(b).

a S.No.	b Category. of college teachers	c Number Agreeing.	d Number Undecided.	e Number Disagreed.	f Number of persons who did not expressed any opinion.
1.	Female (39)	25 (64,1)	11 (28.2)	2 (5.1)	1 (2.6)
2.	Male (50)	37 (74)	10 (20)	1 (2)	2 (4)

The degree of support expressed in the case of the statement that moral education should be imparted in colleges is considerably more both by female and male college-teachers than the overall support given by the general group. College students themselves (of both sexes) also expressed considerable support to the idea of providing moral education in our educational institutions while reacting to statement S-1.

In the case of statement 13(c), maximum agreement was expressed by the income-group having a monthly income of Rs. 4000 and above. Starting with this, as we come to the sub-groups with lower monthly incomes, the degree of agreement to this statement successively decreases. May be that the people with higher incomes have a better appreciation of the role of mass-media on account of their greater exposure to these media.

Conditioners of Human Behaviour :

It would be desirable to briefly mention here some basic factors which influence our thought and behaviour pattern.

(i) *Samskaras or Natural Tendencies*: Every person is born with certain propensities, likes and dislikes, potentialities — inherited or otherwise. The ancient thinkers of India called them samskaras or impressions accumulated by an individual spirit in its previous births. All this is called individual's inherent nature which differs from person to person. The nature of an individual plays an important role in determining his or her behaviour.

(ii) *Education and Environment*: It may be dificult to say if an individual's nature or his nurture plays a greater role in shaping the individual's conduct; but it goes without saying that nurture in the form of education and environmental influences have a significant impact in shaping the character of a person.

(iii) *Free Will*: Every individual is endowed with a 'free-will'. By exercising his free-will an individual becomes the architect of his own destiny.

Every individual, when he enters this world, brings with him a set of samskaras— impressions, tendencies, and attitudes. As he goes through his life, by the process of education and interaction with various situations in the social milieu, he acquires new samskaras and his old samaskaras get modified. With the judicious application of one's free-will, every individual raises the behavioural edifice of one's life and becomes the architect of his own future.

Character Training : A Historical Perspective

History of education reveals that in ancient times, say upto the 6th century AD, many countries laid considerable emphasis on character-training of the young children. In India, religion emphasised ethical conduct, art, literature, jurisprudence etc. In Rome, cultivating respect for traditions, austerity and frugality was an important function of education. Character-training was a salient feature of the Mayan education. Chinese regarded moulding of character a prime concern of education. Zoroastrians, in ancient Persia, attached considerable importance tc training the young in practices of good thoughts, good words and good actions. Byzantine system of education went even to the extent of mostly confining itself to religious instruction to students and encouraging among them asetic practices and thus developing in them an attitude of indifference towards secular subjects. Athens, the cultural centre of ancient Greece, was known for the stress it laid on moral training of the youth and cultivating good conduct and grace in them. Sparta in Greece, besides training the youth (from the age of seven) in physical culture, taught them the art of lying and theft etc. as these were some of the values with the Spartans. Spartan morality, however, demanded that this kind of Machiavallianism was to be practised only while dealing with the foreigners.

During the medieval India, when there was Islamic rule in the country, maktabs, *i.e.* institutions of early education taught the students to say their daily prayers as indicated in the Holy Quran. In the institutions of higher learning i.e. madrassas, Hadit was taught. A number of denominational schools in India still teach students religious practices of their respective faiths. Bible discourse is still compulsory in the schools of England. In Russia after the great Revolution character was attempted to be moulded through the teachings of communism.

Role of Educational Institutions

Educational institutions constitute the biggest organised sector for imparting various kinds of training, including moral training, to the growing youths. As regards the stage at which moral education programme should begin in the educational institutions, Meriel Downey says :

"It (moral development) is an area to which no pupil comes 'cold', since moral learning, the development of values and attitudes begins at birth and is fed from many sources. For this reason, it is not something that can be delayed, like, say, the learning of Latin, until we feel that pupils have reached an appropriate stage of mental development to cope with the demands which it will make upon their intellectual abilities".[2]

A number of people are of the view that moral education, in the school system, should begin from the pre-primary stage so that students develop proper samskaras and attitudes from the early years of their lives.

Official Documents on Moral Education

It would be relevant to study the views of various commissions and committees on the subject of moral education.

(a) **Pre-independence period**

(i) The Education Commission of 1882 had recommended that, based upon the fundamental principles of natural religion, an attempt be made to prepare a text-book on moral education. This book should be taught in all Government and non-Government colleges. The principal or one of the professors in each Government and aided colleges should deliver a series of lectures to all the classes on the duties of a man and a citizen.

The Government, however, rejected the proposal by its Resolution No. 10/309 of October 2, 1884.

(ii) Thereafter a significant recommendation in this regard was made in the Memorandum of the Post-War Educational Development (1944). The recommendation runs as follows:

"Religion in the widest sense, should inspire all education and that a curriculum devoid of an ethical basis will prove barren in the end".

(iii) The Religious Education Committee of the Central Advisory Board of Education (CABE) recommended in 1945, "Spiritual and moral teachings common to all religions should be an integral part of the curriculum and provision/facilities for instructions therein should be the responsibility of the State."

(b) Post-independence Period

(i) The 42nd Constitutional Amendment of 1976, inserted as Article 51A in Part IVA of the Indian Constitution lays down ten Fundamental Duties (or values) for each citizen. This amendment was inspired by the idea of arresting the falling moral standards in the country and that of ensuring higher level of moral conduct from the citizens.

(ii) The University Education Commission (1948-49) recommended that:

"unless morality is taken in a larger sense, it is not enough. If we exclude spiritual training in our institutions we would be untrue to our whole historical development".[3]

(iii) The Secondary Education Commission (1952-53) asserted that 'religious and moral instruction' played an important role in the growth of individual's character.

(iv) Sri Prakasa Committee on Religious and Moral Instruction (1959) held the view that -

" Many ills that our world of education and our society as a whole is suffering from, resulting in wide-spread disturbance and dislocation of life, are mainly due to gradual disappearance of the hold of basic principles of religion on the hearts of the people---The only cure, it seems to us, is in deliberate inculcation of moral and spiritual values from the earliest years of our lives." [5]

(v) The subject was also dealt with by the Indian Education Commission (1964-66), which recommended -

"conscious and organised attempts be made for imparting education in social, moral and spiritual values with the help, wherever possible, of ethical teachings of great religions".[6]

(vi) Challenge of Education (1985), published by the Union Ministry of Education, summed up the position in this regard as follows:

"Thoughtful people in all walks of life are greatly disturbed by a progressive erosion of values and the resultant pollution of public life. The fact that this crisis of values is as pervasive in schools, colleges and universities, amongst teachers as well as students as in other walks of life, is seen as a highly dangerous development. It is, therefore, being urged that the process of education should be reoriented and young people should be made to realise that exploitation, insecurity and violence cannot be contained nor can an organised society be sustained without adhering to and enforcing some norms of social, political and economic behaviour. Learning from past experience, it is expected that a coherent and an operationally viable value-system would be inculcated through educational process, based upon rational and scientific and moral approach to life".[7]

(vii) The Document on Approach to the Seventh Five Year Plan (1985-90) published in July 1984, states, " Value-orientation in education should constitute a special thrust in the Seventh Plan, teacher-education in particular being reoriented for this purpose".

Approaches to Moral Instruction

(1) At the boy-hood stage, individual's physical propensities have a full play; during manhood and old-age intellectual and spiritual values start dominating the corporeal values. Therefore, while imparting moral education, educators must keep this fact in view and no attempt be made to burden the students with intellectual exercises in moral education during early years of their lives.

(2) Value-perspective may be two-dimensional or three-dimensional. A two-dimensional view is caring for oneself as well as for the other because both need each other and any transgression of values may harm both sides. U.S.A. and U.S.S.R. had been very unfriendly till the eighties of this century; but both have respected each other's sovereignty because either of these countries could destroy the other with the pile of destructive weapons it possessed. This kind of need and reciprocity-based value-system would be followed by many people. When the value-system is ideal-based as well, it becomes a three-dimensional value system. The three-dimensional value-system can be followed over a long period of time by a few persons only.

(3) The Education Commission (1964-66) suggested that social, moral and spiritual values should be imparted both through indirect and direct methods. The Commission remarked," We attach great importance to the role of indirect influence in building up good character. The school atmosphere, the personality and behaviour of the teachers, the facilities provided in the school, will have a large say in developing a sense of values. We would like to

emphasise that the consciousness of values must permeate the whole curriculm and programme of activities in the school. It is not only the teachers incharge of moral instruction who are responsible for building character. Every teacher, whatever be the subject he teaches, must necessarily accept this responsibility. —The school assembly, the curricular and co-curricular activities, the celebration of religious festivals of all religions, work-experience, team games and sports, subject clubs, social service programmes — all these can help in inculcating the values of cooperation and mutual regard, honesty and integrity, discipline and social responsibility. These values have a special significance in Indian society today, when young men and women are passing through a crisis of character".[8]

In regard to direct moral instruction, agreeing with the recommendations of the Sri Prakasa Committee, the Commission stated that " one or two periods a week should be set aside in the school time-table for instruction in moral and spiritual values".

At the early school-stages, moral instruction can be imparted through parables or stories which have an appeal to the emotions of the child. At the secondary stage, there can be discussions between the teacher and the taught on the values to be imparted, thus resorting to an intellectual approach to the subject. According to V.K.R.V. Rao, one time Union Education Minister," Ethics should be taught only through parables, stories, religion, and sayings of great people and their lives. Right from the start, children should be taught about the founders of great religions of India. Films should be shown to them depicting temples, mosques, gurudwaras etc."[9]

(4) In ancient times, some states imparted moral education through edicts or some other forms of permanent writings. For example, the Romans expected the children to learn by heart the Twelve Tables of laws. The Japanese employed the imperial edicts for this purpose. One example of the edict is given below.

"Know ye, our subjects :

"Our imperial ancestors have founded our Empire on a basis broad and everlasting and have deeply and firmly implanted virtue; our subjects, ever united in loyalty and filial piety, have from generation to generation illustrated the beauty thereof. This is the glory and the fundamental character of our Empire, and herein also lies the source of our education. Ye, our subjects, be filial to your parents, affectionate to your brothers and sisters; as husbands and wives be harmonious; as friends true; bear yourselves in modesty and moderation; extend your benevolence to all; pursue learning and cultivate arts, and thereby develop intellectual faculties and perfect moral powers; furthermore, advance public good and promote common interests; always respect the Constitution and observe the laws; should emergency arise, offer yourselves courageously to the state; and thus guard and maintain the prosperity of our imperial throne coeval with heaven and earth. So shall ye not only be our good and faithful subjects, but render illustrious the best traditions of your forefathers." [10]

(5) In the teaching of moral practices, both theory and practice are of equal significance, because cognition, feelings and action are interdependent. The quality and depth of information and its sources — all play an important role in influencing our attitudes. Without a proper conceptual background, all action may be reduced to a blind ritual only. However, translation of information into proper action is of great importance, because simple parroting of Ten Commandments cannot make a Moses of an individual. Emphasising the superiority of example over precept, N.K. Dutt says :

"Albert Camus once experimented with inculcation of moral values through teaching. He encouraged students to write an essay on 'Truthfulness'. The best essay was written by the biggest liar of the class. He further said that if the purpose of education is merely to impart information and skills, then thanks to the present day teaching technology, perhaps an idiot can teach another idiot calculus." [11]

The same remarks apply to speech-making also. A person may play a big hoax on the people by play of words and thus claim to be a big preacher of values whereas his own actions may be just the opposite of what he might say.

N.K. Dutt adds that according to Mao-Tse-Tung, "The thoughts of intellectuals are like arrows in a quiver which scratch the back but never fly".[12]

(6) Value orientation is a continuous process. As man evolves intellectually and otherwise, his expectations also get modified. This is true in regard to values also. Society's expectations rise in respect of moral values also, therefore imparting of value-education and adjustment to values should be a continuous process.

Mass-Media and Moral Education

Apart from the educational institutions mass media, *i.e.* media which have the potential to transmit messages to the masses at large, can play a far-reaching role in any scheme of imparting value education — formal, nonformal or informal. Some of these media are privately owned and independent of the government whereas others are directly under the government machinery. Although some government departments bring out various kinds of journals etc., but by and large press and publications in India are free of government control. Some of the mass media under the Union Government are television, radio, Department of Field Publicity, Publication Division, Department of Advertising and Visual Publicity and Song and Drama Division. Though there is a Films Division under the Union Ministry of Information and Broadcasting, it produces documentaries only. Feature-films production is totally in the private sector and this medium is very powerful in influencing the attitudes of the people.

One may, of course, argue that in India mass-media have not been the mass media in the real sense — some of the reasons for this being as follows:

According to 1981 census, India had nearly 140 million families and only 25 million radios and one million TV sets. If TV sets are possessed by the same 25 million who own the radio sets, the reach of these two media is only to 17.9 per cent population and if the TV sets are considered to have been owned by some who own the radio sets and some who do not own the radio set, even then the reach of these two media is to a maximum population of 18.6 per cent of the country's population. The total circulation of newspapers and journals in India is around ten million which comes to less than 1.5 per every hundred people. As nearly half the population in the country is still illiterate, the newspapers and journals have a limited impact on the education of the masses. One may agree that the mass media are not able to reach the vast masses of India inhabiting the length and breadth of the country, yet they have, admittedly a great potential of wielding a considerable influence on human minds, therefore these media can be gainfully employed in the moral education programme.

It is, thus, observed that there is a general consensus that moral education should be imparted in our educational institutions as well as through the mass-media. Various commissions and committees on education have been stressing the need for social, moral and spiritual education programme being introduced in our educational institutions. Any programme of value-education must take into account the age and other factors of the target population. The programme, in order to be useful, should lay equal emphasis on precept and practice. The character of the teacher or any other person imparting moral education is of greater significance than his precepts as actions always speak louder than the words and the totality of the educator's personality is far more important than his utterances, howsoever loud and pious these might be. Mass media, which have a deep and powerful influence on human minds, should also devise a well-planned programme in respect of moral education and thus contribute to resolving the present crisis of character in the society.

References and Notes

1. *The Statesman*, New Delhi; July 26, 1988, p.8
2. Downey Meriel and Kelley A V; *Moral Education; Theory and Practice*, Harper and Row, London, p.vii.
3. Report of the University Education Commission (1948-49).
4. Radhakrishnan S; *Eastern Religion and Western Thought.*
5. *Documents on social, Moral and Spiritual Values in Education*, National Council of Educational Research and Training (NCERT), New Delhi, 1979, p.23.
6. Report of the Education Commission (1964-66), para 8.94.
7. *Challenge of Education — a Policy Perspective;* Ministry of Education, Government of India, New Delhi; 1985, para 1.24.
8. Report of the Education Commission (1964-66); para 8.95.
9. *National Integration Council Papers* for the First meeting on Thursday, June 20, and Friday, June 21, 1968 at Srinagar, Government of India, Ministry of Home Affairs, New Delhi. p.20.
10. Baron Kikuchi in Myers Philip Van Ness; *History As Past Ethics — An Introduction to the History of Morals;* (Boston: Gin and Company, 1913, p.92.
11. Dutt N.K. in Ruhela SP (ed); *Human Values and Education;* Sterling Publishers Pvt. Ltd., New Delhi, Bangalore; 1986,p.14.
12. *Ibid.*

4

The Role of Religion

The Concise Oxford Dictionary defines religion as a "particular system of faith and worship — human recognition of superhuman controlling power and especially of a personal God or Gods entitled to obedience and worship". The main components of any religion are theology, rituals and code of conduct. However, there are some religions which are not theo-centric.

It is believed that in India, the conception of Supreme Being, the first cause of the universe i.e., the Brahma, had a great impact on the moral code of the Aryans. Starting from the worship of various elements of nature such as the sky, the earth and various forces of nature, there was a trend towards finding unity in them. Polytheism was correlated to monotheism just as forces of nature namely, heat, light, electricity to one single thing 'energy'. This Single Cause of the universe, was impersonal, absolute, passionless and beyond consciousness, just like energy in this material world, is the primal cause of the universe. This chain of thought led our ancestors to one of the greatest philosophical conceptions — that the whole world was one. This concept is as important today as it was any time in the past.

The concept of religion is bound to vary from person to person and from society to society. For example, in Hinduism, the equivalent of religion is 'dharma', which is far more a comprehensive word than the word religion. The word 'dharma' is from the root 'dhra', which means something which holds the society and this universe together. As such,'dharma' lays greater stress on one's goals, functions, obligations and duties. It is, difficult to say which the conception of religion (which) the respondents had in mind when reacting to the following statement:

" It would be appropriate to impart moral education,

(a) Without reference to religious teachings;

or

(b) With reference to teachings in various religions.(G-2)

Religion and Moral Teaching

Option	No.of Persons Agreeing.	No. of persons Disagreeing.	No. Undecided
(a)	382 (43.3)	7 (0.8)	
or			19 (2.2)
(b)	469 (53.2)	4 (0.5)	

Positive Role of Religion: Thus more than 50 per cent of the respondents favoured moral education with reference to religious teachings. There could be several reasons for it, some of which may be as follows:

(i) Religion plays a positive role in the moral uplift of man. It may, at times, be the fear of gods which may be the motive factor for individual's right conduct. William Newton Clarke considered the role of religion in imparting moral education as that of a school master. He wrote in his book 'The Christian Doctrine of God'.

" Doubtless the ethical life of the world has suffered much from religion, but it owes to religion immeasureably more than it has suffered from it. Faulty enough indeed the influence has been, but the ethical life of the world has on the whole been greatly reinforced and purified by its religions."[1]

(ii) All religions are creations of superb minds. Religious writings are replete with episodes which have great moral lessons for man. It would be lack of wisdom on the part of man not to benefit from the wealth of experience stored in the religious books.

(iii) We, in India, are not trying to create an irreligious society. What we have accepted is a variously religious society, and not a society which has nothing to do with religion. Therefore, religion cannot be rejected merely on the ground that we are a secular state.

Negative Role of Religion

Those who are opposed to assigning any role to religion in the sphere of moral education may have some of the following arguments in mind.

(i) According to Article 28 (1) of the Constitution of India,

"No religious instruction shall be provided in any educational institution wholly maintained out of State Fund."

This, of course, does not apply to the educational institutions run by private trusts. In regard to such institutions, Article 28(3) of the Constitution lays down the following policy.

"No person attending any educational institution recognised by the State or receiving aid out of State funds shall be required to take part in any religious instruction that may be imparted in such institutions or to attend any religious worship that may be conducted in such institutions or in any premises attached thereto unless such person or, if such a person is a minor, his guardian has given his consent thereto."

(ii) Religion is identified by some people more as theology, a set of rituals, fear of God and greed for heaven rather than a code of conduct evolved over a period of years. Such people see no link between religion and morality. In his work '*Christianity and Hinduism*, Bishop Caldwell writes,

"We meet with a moral Hindu who has broken altogether away from religion and, what is still more common, still more extraordinary, we meet with a devout Hindu who lives a flagrantly immoral life. In the latter case no person sees any inconsistency between immorality and devoutnes."[2]

'The Karma Theory' which is one of the fundamental principles of Hinduism proclaims the importance of virtuous acts. The following legend in a Hindu sacred-book brings out very aptly the higher place of a kind act than the performance of rituals. A rich man, once, performed the ritual of offering 1000 mangoes to the sacred Ganges. One of these mangoes was picked up by a poor beggar to satisfy his hunger. The same night, the rich man, in his dream saw the goddess Ganges who told him that she had accepted the offering of one mango only! The 'devout Hindus' of Caldwell experience are therefore, not truly religious.

(iii) People project their moral conceptions in the shape of gods; but once created these divinities react on the conscience of their creators. Examples are not wanting where divinities created by the priest class and other powerful sections in the society have had an adverse influence on the morals of the society. It is in the name of some divinities that injustices are perpetrated on the weaker sections of the society.

(iv) To many people, religion has meant forcible proselytisation at the point of bayonet or economic and social exploitation of others. Religions have led to feuds among the co-religionists as well as between people of different faiths.

(v) Communists as well as many other people have no faith in any religion. Religions like Buddhism make no reference to God. If moral teachings are to be based on religion, it would amount to imparting no moral education to persons who do not believe in religion.

(vi) Some of these people hold that moral education should be based on rational thinking only. In ancient Greece, where there was no priestly class, the country had no theocratic morality. Aristotle discussed only scientific foundations of morality. In ancient Rome, morality was based on patriotism and not religion.

(vii) The great Hindu codifier of values, Manu, makes no reference to rituals and supernatural things in his definition of dharma.[3]

Those who hold that moral education should be imparted independent of religion argue that if some day a person rejects his religion (and this can happen with the growth of materialistic values), he would reject morality also. It would, in a way, amount to throwing the baby along with the bath tub.

(viii) Today, many societies are pluralistic and have a markedly different value-system arising from their respective religions. Therefore, there is an inherent difficulty in linking morality with religion.

Critics and scholars have also pointed towards several disintegrating factors in various religions. For example, Judaism, Christianity and Islam, which have a common catchment area, believe in an exclusive God. Their God brooks no rival, whereas according to Hinduism, all Gods are manifestation of the same Brahma; only the sages have described Him differently. The Judaic God commands his worshippers that when they enter the land of their enemies, they will "destroy their altars, and break their images, and cut down their groves, and burn their graven images with fire".

(Bible, Deut 7.5). Iconoclasm, temple razing has been preached and practised by Islam to a similar degree. It is told that Walid was sent by the prophet to destroy the idol of al-Uzza at Nakhle worshipped by the tribal people there. Wherever the followers of Christianity went, they destroyed gods and religious places of the 'non-believers'. "When America was discovered, the Benedictine monks who came in the train of Columbus boasted of having destroyed single-handed 170,000 images in Haiti alone. Juan de Zummarage, the first Bishop of Mexico, writing as early as 1531 claimed that he destroyed 500 temples and 20,000 idols of the heathens. In our own country, in Goa, Jesuit fathers destroyed many Hindu temples".[9] The Hindus, at one time, had to pay 'Jazia', only because they were Hindus and not Muslims. A law laid down that infidels could not build their temples. The Laxmi Narain Temple in New Delhi is reported to have come up in the country after a lapse of about 700 years.[10] Various religions, thus, appear to have been reduced to mere denominations only.

Via-Media

In case educational institutions adopt an attitude of indifference to religion, it would mean leaving the interpretation of religion to the reactionaries and half-educated people only and jeopardising the process of social evolution.

The works of the religiously inclined saints and sufi poets and philosophers like Namdev, Tukaram, Kabir, Kurral, Jaisi, S. Radhakrishnan and others in different languages express moral truths in epigramatic phrases. All such works have had a great moralising influence on the society and it would be a mistake not to make use of them for their literary and moral value.

Every religion lays down some code of conduct for its followers and contains in its books numerous legends to inspire its faithfuls to observe certain norms of behaviour. It would be useful to make use of this heritage for imparting ethical education to students.

Each religion preaches spiritual fulfilment, withdrawing from the lower pulls to higher recesses of mind, prayer, meditation, inculcation of virtues like compassion, contentment, good actions, self-surrender, service of mankind and all that can elevate man and the society.

Whatever be the source of the material employed for moral education, all discussions on the value-system should be on rational basis only and not wrapped in meaningless myths and superstitions. For example, it would be an incorrect approach to say, 'Respect women because it is written in Manusmriti.[4]

यत्र नार्यस्तु पूज्यन्ते रमन्ते तत्र देवताः
यत्रैतास्तु न पूज्यन्ते सर्वास्तत्रफलाः क्रियाः

(yatra nariastu poojante, ramante tatra devata,
yatraiatastu na poojante, sarvaatatraphala kriya).

'Homes where women are worshipped become the abode of gods but where women are not given respect, all the actions of the people there end up in failure'.

Instead, students should be told with examples that whenever and wherever women have been given an opportunity in education, services or other spheres, their contribution has been no less than that of men. On this account as well as on account of the sacrifice which women make as mothers, they are worthy of great respect.

It would be wrong to attribute some of the existing social ills solely to religion. Foreign aggressions, alien rule, present day consumerism and absence of developmental work over long periods—are vital factors responsible for moral decay of the society.

Religious Codes of Conduct

To the statement that —

" Students should be given an intelligent understanding of the codes of conduct of various religions", (G-9), the respondents reacted as follows.

S.No.	Category of Respondents	Number Agreeing	Number Undecided	Number Disagreed	Number of persons who expressed no opinion
1	2	3	4	5	6
1	Total population (881)	798 (90.6)	39 (4.4)	44 (5)	-
2.	Age-Group 18-25 years (52)	43 (82.7)	4 (7.7)	5 (9.6)	-
3.	Above 40 years (574)	532 (92.7)	20 (3.5)	22 (3.8)	-
4.	High School & equivalent (123)	115 (3,5)	1 (0.8)	7 (5.7)	-

1	2	3	4	5	6
5.	MA or above and equivalent (464)	414 (89.2)	27 (5.8)	23 (5)	-
6.	With income from Rs. 1000-1999 p.m (98)	88 (89.8)	6 (6.1)	4 (4.1)	-
7.	With income of Rs. 4000 p.m. and above (407)	369 (90.7)	16 (3.9)	22 (5.4)	-

All the categories of respondents listed above lent a high degree of support to the statement.

Religion has played a central role and is still playing an important role in the life of the Indian people. All our works of ancient art, literature, dance, music, etc. are intimately interwoven with religious myths and thought. Sciences such as astronomy and geometry etc. were cultivated in India initially for religious purposes only. Therefore, it may not be possible to eliminate religion from our lives without the grave risk of cutting ourselves from our roots. According to a news-report, a record number of 19.92 lakhs pilgrims visited the holy shrine of Vaishno Devi during 1988, exceeding the previous year's mark by 1.35 lakhs. These pilgrims came from all over India.[5] On the New Year Day of 1989, the income of the holy Venketeshwar Temple at Tirumala Tirupati was Rs. 26.54 lakhs which was Rs.2.39 lakhs more than the previous year's income on this day.[6] Even a number of politicians who swear by secularism visit the holy shrines located all over India. The visit by these leaders may be politically motivated, but they indicate the 'direction of the wind' in our country. Due to great appeal which religion has for the Indian masses, religion was used as an effective weapon during the freedom struggle of the country. V. Subramaniam writes—

"Annie Besant's use of the Bhagvadgita and theosophy appealed to the urban high-caste Hindu — while Tilak widened the base of appeal through using the Ganesh Puja as an instrument of politico-cultural revivalism quite apart from his Karmayogic (activist) reinterpretation of the Bhagvadgita. Bengali radicalism drew inspiration from the Mother Goddess right from its early days — and Gandhiji's efforts to appeal to the widest public included the slogan of Ram Rajya and the singing of Ram Dhun. In short, the nationalist movement though never exclusively Hindu nor theocratic, nevertheless used Hindu religion cultural symbols and slogans as the most practical instruments of mobilisation of the Indians — inspite of strong criticism both from the Right and Left, from Liberals such as Sapru or Kunzru and Leftists such as Jawahar Lal Nehru, the Congress Socialists and the Communists."[7]

The motif 'Yoga is efficiency in action' '(Yoga Karmasu Kaushlam), adopted by the National Academy of Administration and the National Productivity Counil is from the holy Bhagvad-gita. Of course, the choice of the motif would have been on account of its appropriateness and eloquence and not religious considerations but this is all the more reason that the students should be given an intelligent understanding of various religions and the useful messages contained in the religious text.

" The Indians," remarks Sir Harcourt Butler," are as essentially religious as the Europeans are essentially secular. Religion is still the beginning and the end, the alpha and omega of Indian Life".— " This belief finds expression in a bitter satire of the Urdu poet Akbar, of which the gist is " The East is spiritual, the West is material. Mansur (the Sufi Pantheist who was executed in Baghdad in AD 922 for blasphemy) declared, 'I am God.' Darwin announced " I am the son of an ape".[8]

Role of Religious Institutions :

As regards the role of the religious institutions, the questionnaire for the students carried the following statement.

"Religious institutions such as temples, mosques, churches should play greater role in propagating moral values in the society". (S-11)

Value-Dissemination By Religious Institutions :

a	b	c	d	e	f
S.No.	Category. of Respondents	Number Agreeing.	Number Undecided.	Number Disagreeing.	Number of persons who expressed no opinion.
(1)	Total population of students. (267)	182 (68.2)	33 (12.3)	52 (19.5)	

a	b	c	d	e	f
(2)	School students (M) (70)	48 (68.6)	6 (8.6)	16 (22.8)	
(3)	School students (F) (86)	51 (59.3)	19 (22.1)	16 (18.6)	-
(4)	College students (M) (34)	25 (73.5)	3 (8.3)	6 (17.7)	-
(5)	College students (F) (7)	51 (72.9)	5 (7.1)	14 (20)	-
(6)	College students (M) from Africa in Delhi colleges. (7)	7 (100)	-	-	-
(7)	Total population of Indian students (when students from Africa are not included in the total population.) (260)	175 (67.3)	33 (12.7)	52 (20)	-

The above score-chart leads us to two inferences.[10]

(a) College students agree with the statement to a greater degree than do the school students.

(b) Male students are more in favour of the idea that the religious institutions should play a greater role in propagating moral values than the female students.

(c) In each case the degree of agreement with the statement is less than 75 per cent.

More than 25 per cent of the respondents were undecided on this issue or were opposed to the idea of religious institutions taking up the work of the propagation of moral values, possibly due to the fact that the respondents were skeptical about the ability of the religious institutions to achieve results. Some of the following steps could be considered for equipping the religious institutions for working effectively in the sphere of value-education.

(i) It should be ensured that the temple-priests or other similar personnel involved in the work take a progressive and not an obscurant's view of religion. For this purpose, a system would have to be evolved on a national basis for entry to priesthood. Individuals wishing to become priest should go through an adequate course of training and education. In the USSR. prior to glasnost and perestroika, notwithstanding that communism is antagonistic to religion, the priests, before they could take up priesthood, have had to go through a course of adequate training and education in religious and other allied texts. If government can successfully intervene with the administration of the Vaishnu Devi temple in J and K State, there is no reason why a similar system cannot be introduced or at least experimented in India.

(ii) The education programme of the priests must drill the trainees in the concept of oneness of the Supreme Being and certain degree of the comparative study of various religions. Ahura Mazada in Zoroastrianism, Allah in Islam, Heavenly Father in Christianity, Iswara in Hinduism, and Sunyata in Buddhism are only different names given by different people in different geographical and linguistic regions for the same cosmic, creative, infinite and eternal energy. The leaders of religious institutions should be trained to remain free from bigotry.

(iii) The people in religious institutions, like all other people, should bear in mind that as a society evolves intellectually, spiritually and socially, its value-system undergoes a metamorphosism. In case religious institutions refuse to accept this logic, they would lose their credibility. A couple of examples of a progressive and a rational approach in this regard are given here.

Example-I : Among the Muslims it was held for a long time that the *Zakat* or the *Wakf*, i.e., the money collected for charity purposes, is to be spent, among other things, for religious education only as distinct from secular education. In recent years, rational Muslims have justified the utilisation of *Zakat* for secular education. According to these 'progressive thinkers',the Holy prophet Mohammad had sent a number of people to India and China to receive education. Evidently these people had not gone to these countries to receive Quranic education. Therefore, it is perfectly in accordance with the Islamic thought to utilise *Wakf* for imparting secular education.

Example-II: Islamic text, on theocratic basis, divides the world into two sections — *Dar-al-islam* and Dar-al-*Harb** It was said that no taxes be levied by Muslim countries for imports from the former category of countries whereas taxes may be levied in the case of the second category. The rationalist Muslims have, in recent years, changed this view in this manner. They say that Islam upholds the essentiality of survival. As money is necessary for survival, therefore taxes may be levied in the case of all categories including the first category.

Example-III: According to Islam, Muslims are not allowed to charge interest from anyone, even from banks. The modern thinking among some Muslims is that banks invest money-deposits of the individuals in various projects and business deals and earn profits. As sharing of profits is not specifically banned by islam, the depositors can accept these profits. The issue is still a debatable one as Muslims of the conventional views that trade has an element of profit and loss and risk. As bank deposits do not have this elemental, bank interest cannot be equated to trade profits. They argue that this is a circuitous way of accepting the bank-interest by changing its nomenclature; but then if religious leaders refuse to accept these changes, the changing society would just ignore them and their sermons as well.

Religious Programmes and Mass Media

There was the following statement in the questionnaire relating to mass-media.

"Indu and Joginder Singh were discussing radio and T.V. coverage of such programmes which are religious in character. Indu justified such coverage whereas Joginder Singh felt that such

* (i) Dar-al-Islam : Abode of peace. A country ruled by Muslims by Islamic laws.

(ii) Dar-al-Harb : Abode of war. A country not under the Muslim rule and against which Muslims should carry out 'jihad' i.e., the holy war.

The above terms were envolved by the Muslim jurists. Technically speaking, there is no country in the world today ruled strictly by the Islamic laws, hence there is no Dar-al-Islam. As there is no country also, where Muslims are debarred from performing their fundamental duties such as Zarat, Fasting and Prayers. There is no Dar-al-Harb either. In the terminology of these Muslim jurists, India is Dar-al-Aman, where Muslims have all the freedom to perform their fundamental duties; but they are not in majority here. Loosely speaking some Middle East Countries and Pakistan can be listed as Dar-al-Islam.

coverage violated the principle of secularism. Who, in your opinion, was correct?

(a) Indu, who favoured such coverage;

OR

(b) Joginder, who opposed such coverage. (G-10)

Coverage of Religious Programmes

A	B	C	D
Option	No. and percentage of persons Agreeing.	No. Disagreeing.	No. Undecided
(a)	531 (60.3)	5 (0.6)	68 (7.7)
(b)	274 (31.1)	3 (0.3)	

The above statistics show that nearly double the number supported coverage of religious programmes by mass media as compared to those who opposed it. The proponents of (a) above may justify their stand on the following grounds :

(a) Preventing the mass-media from doing such a coverage would, to some extent, mean working for a closed society. The endeavour, on the contrary, should be to depict all religions, cultures as well as sub-cultures rather than drawing a curtain on them. India's mission to evolve a society with composite culture and not one which is indifferent to all cultures.

(b) Any belief or custom which becomes a part of the main-stream of life no longer remains exclusively religious. It becomes a part of the social life of the community and deserves to be depicted by the mass-media. The immense popularity of the Ramayana and the Mahabharata T.V. serials from the Doordarshan net-work amply establishes the justification of projecting such programmes through the mass-media.

(c) Secularism has two forms. There is the 'absolute secularism' which is practised in the communist world where religion has no place in the planned affairs of the country. There the religion is a totally private affair.

The Indian view of secularism is, however, different. In India, all religions can flourish. The government does not give preferential treatment to any particular religion. Therefore, if a balanced coverage of important programmes of all religions is undertaken by mass-media, it would lead to better understanding of all cultures by different communities inhabiting the country.

Those opposed to the use of mass-media for religious programmes primarily may be of the opinion that the Preamble of the Indian Constitution declares India a secular state, therefore the government should not dabble with religion. They may be interpreting secularism as communist societies do this. Some persons in this category also have a feeling that the government mass-media occasionally, give a preferential treatment to the programmes of one religion vis-a-vis programmes of other religions. Difficult as it may be to totally ward off such an imbalance or an error of judgement in the selection of programmes for the mass-media, its incidence can be reduced by drawing up a clear and a well-thought out policy. The question is which is more hazardous in a multi-cultural society—to deprive the people of the chance of having an intelligent understanding of the cultures and religions of other communities and interaction with them or taking a calculated risk of the consequences which would flow if there is some error in the choice of programmes for dissemination through mass-media. Perhaps, the latter course may be a better choice.

Conclusion:

It may be argued that human-kind had started observing some kind of moral code earlier than it evolved any kind of religion. Merial Downey and Av Kelley held that:

" -----morality has to be seen independent of religion. If there is a connection it is not that morality is dependent on religious beliefs, it is much more likely that man's religious beliefs are a result of his moral awareness"? As Kant said," Belief in God is grounded in moral consciousness rather than moral law on belief in God."[11]

The question, however, is not if the moral code preceded the evolution of religion or it was the viceversa; but whether in the present context moral education should be undertaken with or without reference to religion. In this context two things are to be kept in view:

(a) Have we evolved adequate secular literature for imparting moral education?

(b) If religion is divorced from theology and belief in supernaturalism, is there any harm if its moral code, and fables, stories and other relevant material are used for imparting moral education?

In this connection one cannot overlook that only 53.2 per cent of the respondents supported the application of religion for moral education, whereas 43.3 per cent supported that moral education should be imparted without reference to religious teachings. However, it is not known what was the picture of religion that the respondents had in mind while reacting to this statement? If the picture of religion before them was that of bigoted priests, performance of unmeaningful rituals, sermonising doctrines, one would agree that religious teachings should be kept aloof from moral education; but if religion means harmony of the individual with all forms of life and matter in the cosmos, religion provides a sound basis for moral education.

In view of the above, it would be desireable, as corroborated by about 90 per cent of each category of respondents (in G-9) to give students an intelligent and a rational understanding of the code of conduct of various religions, so that students are not deprived of the wealth of experience stored in these books.

If our dilapidated value-system is to be restructured and saved from decaying further, it is essential that religious establishments should also play their full role in this regard. For this purpose, it would be necessary to have an educated priesthood which has a comprehensive view of various religions and can see the elements of unity behind all religions. The mass-media should also take a balanced and a rational view while projecting customs, traditions and programmes etc., connected with various religions and intended to impart information to the viewers on different aspects of the national and cultural life and for inculcation of moral values among them.

References and Notes

1. Clarke in Myers Philip Van Ness; *History As Past Ethics — An Introduction to The History of Morals;* Boston : Ginn and Company; 1913; p.9
2. Bishop Caldwell in L.S.S.O' Malley; *Hinduism;* Scientific Publishers, Jodhpur, 1985;
3. Surrinder Kumar; *Vishudh Manusmriti;* Arsh Sahitya Prachar Trust, 1986; p.285 (92/62).
4. Ibid, p. 184; (36/56).

5. *Evening News*, New Delhi, January 3, 1989; p.11.
6. *Sandhya Times* (Nav Bharat Times Publication), January 6, 1989; p.1.
7. Subramaniam V; *Cultural Integration in India*; Ashish Publishing House, 1979; p. 171.
8. L.S.S.O'. MALLEY *Hinduism*; Scientific Publishers, Jodhpur, 1985; P. 45.
9. Ram Sarup, *A Need to Face the Truth*, Indian Express, Bangalore, June 18, 1989; p.8.
10. Ibid.
11. Downey Merial and Kelley Av, *Moral Education: Theory and Practice*, Harper and Row, London, p.8.

5

Dissemination of Cultural Heritage

Culture is the level of sophistication achieved by a community in various fields of human activity, including politics, economics, religion, arts, sciences, lilterature etc. There is a fine distinction between civilisation and culture. All that we possess in concrete shape is our civilisation but the abstract permeating the concrete is our culture. The houses that we have, the dress that we wear are parts of our civilisation; but the design and the abstract planning behind them signify our culture. Similarly, the values that we observe in our speech and conduct are the constituents of our culture. All our cultural possession is either a result of our own efforts or it has been passed on to us by our ancestors. As culture is the sum total of the rich experience stretched over centuries of our human existence, there is no reason for us to remain indifferent to it. The Constitution of India, in Article 29 (1), gives every section of the citizens the right to conserve its own culture. Article 51A assigns to every citizen, as one of the Fundamental Duties, 'to value and preserve the rich heritage of our composite culture'. The Union Ministry of Human Resource Development has a full-fledged department as well as a Cultural Heritage Division for the promotion of arts and culture.

Cultural Education

A statement was included in the questionnaire for the general category of respondents to know the public opinion in regard to one of the aspects of the Indian culture. The statement was as follows :

"Indians need to be made better aware of their cultural heritage." (G-6)

The general pattern of responses to the statement is given in the following table:

Awareness of Cultural Heritage

a	b	c	d	e
S.No.	Category of Respondents	No. Agreeing	No. Undecided	No. Disagreeing
(1)	Total population (881)	833 (94.6)	24 (2.7)	24 (2.7)
(2)	Age-group 18-25 years (52)	49 (94.3)	1 (1.9)	2 (3.8)
(3)	Above 40 years (573)	54 (94.4)	17 (3.)	15 (2.6)
(4)	High School & equivalent (123)	118 (96)	2 (1.6)	3 (2.4)
(5)	M.A or above & equivalent (463)	435 (94)	12 (2.6)	16 (3.4)
(6)	With income from Rs. 1000-1999 p.m. (98)	92 (93.9)	5 (5.0)	1 (1.0)
(7)	With income of Rs. 4000 p.m and above. (406)	380 (93.6)	14 (3.4)	12 (3)

More than 90 per cent of respondents in each category have expressed agreement with the statement.

It would be interesting to also study the responses of the student-community to an identical statement which is reproduced below:

"Students should be made aware of Indian culture through history, literature and other books".

(S-6)

The following table sums up the responses of the students :

Culture Dissemination Through Books

a	b	c	d	e
S.No	Category of Respondents	No. Agree-ing	No. Un-decided	No. Dis-agreeing
1.	Total population (267)	256 (96)	6 (2.2)	5 (1.8)
2.	School students (M) (70)	64 (91.4)	3 (4.3)	3 (4.3)
3.	School students (F) (86)	84 (97.7)	0 (0)	2 (2.3)
4.	College-students (M) (34)	33 (97)	1 (3)	0 (0)
5.	College-students(F) (70)	69 (98.6)	1 (1.4)	0 (0)
6.	African students in Indian colleges (M) (7)	6 (85.7)	1 (14.3)	0 (0)

The pattern of students' reaction to this statement is, more or less, similar to the one indicated by the general population to statement G-6, which has been analysed earlier. There are, however, differences in the responses of school-students when compared to those of college-students. Fewer male school students agree with the statement.

Governmental Plans

The Education Commission (1964-66) had urged Indian Universities to ensure "that every student who passes out of an Indian university takes with him some understanding of India's cultural heritage, its past achievements and triumphs in the field of art, philosophy, science and so on. He should, in other words, know what he is heir to. This could perhaps, best be done at the first degree stage where such a study could form a part of a programme of liberal education. It is noteworthy, in this connection, that all university students in America have to take a course in Western civilisation".[1]

The Programme of Action published by the Government of India for implementing the National Policy on Education 1986, elaborates this point at some length in the chapter on 'The Cultural Perspective'. It speaks of several strategies intended for creating better awareness among students of the country's cultural heritage. A few strategies are summed up below:

(a) A suitable hand book should be prepared for the guidance of teachers of each stage of education. Reorientation programmes should be organised for them and audio-visual and other material such as musical instruments, pictures, posters etc., should be prepared for students. A separate room in the school, could be ear-marked for cultural exhibits, wherever it is possible;

(b) One teacher for culture should be provided in each institution.

(c) Distortions in curriculum, particularly in social studies and history should be corrected. Value-orientation should be given to lessons by drawing material from Indian heritage and great classics.

(d) Exhibitions of the work of local artists should be organised.

(e) Students should be encouraged to undertake the conservation of local historical monuments.

(f) Inter-school cultural meets should be arranged so as to bring out India's rich cultural diversity.

The programme of Action makes the following suggestions in this regard for university stage:

(a) Broad-basing and diversifying cultural courses as of fine arts, music, dance, etc.

(b) correction of existing historical and cultural distortion in the courses of study such as of social sciences, humanities and languages etc. In this regard a *tour d' force* would have to be attempted but this is necessary in order to rectify the faulty perspectives;

(c) developing special courses in technical and professional institutions for conservation of monuments which are of immense importance as country's valuable ancient heritage;

(d) forming clubs and societies devoted to the promotion of various cultural aspects;

(e) earmarking incentives, fellowships, scholarships etc. for creative work and research in the field of culture.

Some Dimensions of Curriculum

The dissemination of India's cultural heritage should aim at acquainting students with:

(i) Customs, traditions and festivals etc. of various ethnic, religious and linguistic groups inhabiting the country.

(ii) Works of ancient rishis, sufis, saints, insight into all-time epics, and other great classics.

(iii) Contributions of great men in various fields of the country's national life.

(iv) Cultural wealth contained in our works of religion.

Religion is an important part of the cultural heritage, and more so in the case of India where fine and performing arts and literature have a strong spiritual/religious basis. However, while debating cultural themes related to religion, theocratic education should be excluded.

(v) Intelligent interpretation of myths and poetic fantasies.

Myths form an important part of India's, or for that matter, any culture. Some of the writings described as myths have proved to be meaningful today, whereas other are meant to convey some message to mankind. Pushpak Viman was a myth a century ago; but today one can perceive it as if 'might have been a reality' also. In the great work of the Sufi poet Malik Mohammad Jayasi, the heroine *Padmavat* is found talking to a parrot and the bird is talking to her. This might have been a total myth; but it points towards the level of sensitivity of the people towards birds in those times. In Kalidasa's famous work *Meghdoot,* the clouds are taking the message of a lover to his beloved. It is unbelievable and cannot be taken as truth; but it shows how a poet could conceive nature as part of man and man as part of nature.

The stories in the Puranas may have more or less as much element of imagination as of truth; but such writings have a great cultural significance.

They have been called by Socrates as noble lies and have their place in the cultural heritage of man and deserve attention by framers of the educational curricula.

In this context, we may keep in mind a couple of other things also in mind. Firstly, the study of Buddhism in India can be very much a part of the cultural heritage of India; but study of the Chinese or the Japanese version of Buddhism does not constitute a part and parcel of the Indian cultural heritage, though the merit of these studies otherwisecannot be denied. Secondly, there might be certain aspects of the cultural heritage which could have had their value and importance in the past, but stand invalidated today. For example, the practice of 'devadasis' in some Indian temples had the merit of promoting vestal virgins and dance as a part of worship; but it has degenerated and has become an anachronism today. Similarly, caste which was evolved as a measure to promote professional excellence stands condemned today on account of the infiltration of many evils into it. Any debate on cultural heritage must discuss all such issues objectively and rationally and ought not to unduly support degenerated practices.

Work by Indian Missions Abroad

One of the important functions of the Indian missions in other countries is to project India's image abroad. It is sad to note that our Embassies, High Commissions and Counselates are totally ill equipped for dissemination of India's rich cultural heritage in the countries to which they are accredited. These Missions neither have suitable personnel nor adequate material which could provide information on India's diverse and rich cultural heritage. India needs to follow the example of other countries in this respect and establish richly equipped and properly-functioning cultural centres in all foreign countries. In the present-day world rendered smaller by communication facilities, there is scope for greater interaction between peoples of the world. Widening of the scope of cultural interaction through our embassies is bound to enhance India's prestige.

The popularity and esteem of India's culture in other lands is likely to influence, to a certain degree, the attitude of her own people to their own cultural heritage. Thus the investment in projecting India's culture abroad would serve several purposes, some which include are —

(a) a boost in India's prestige, as her cultural achievements excel most rather all countries of the world;

(b) infusion of a sense of self-esteem among the peope of India and thus also lead to greater enthusiasm among the Indians for imbibing their own cultural values;

(c) dissemination of India's cultural message for the benefit of mankind as was done by her predecessors in South East Asia, China, Japan, Mexico and elsewhere.

Conclusion:

Culture is the totalilty of thoughts, symbols, beliefs, sentiments etc. which a group has developed and refined over a period of time and with which it has enriched its material life. Indian culture, broadly speaking, has material spiritual/intellectual aspects. The historical remains and ancient writings testify to India's material progress since times immemorial. The Vedas, and the Upanishadas which are the oldest philosophical works in possessions of mankind today indicate the occupation of the Indian mind with the intellectual and spiritual aspects of culture. Hegal says, "A civilisation without a philosophy is like a temple without the holy of the holies". The spectulative aspect of Indian culture first dived into the mystries of nature, as in the Vedas, and thereafter it tried to unravel the mystry of man, universe, matter and energy through the Vedanta. In this connection, Max Muller writes in his work 'Six Systems of Indian Philosophy' (p. 182) :

"It is surely astounding that such a system as the Vendanta should have been slowly elaborated by the indefatigable and intrepid thinkers of India thousands of years ago, a system that even now makes us feel giddy, as in mouting the last steps of the swaying spire of an ancient Gothic Cathedral. None of our philosophers, not excepting Heraclitus, Plato, Kant, or Hegel has ventured to erect such a spire, never frightened by storms or lightnings. Stone follows on stone after regular succession after once the first step has been made, after once it has been clearly seen that in the beginning there can have been but one, as there will be but one in the end, whether we call it Atman or Brahman,"[3]

On the glory of the Upanishadas, Schopenhauer says," In the whole world, there is no study so beneficial and so elevating as that of the Upanishadas. They are destined sooner or later to become the faith of the people."[4]

According to Deussen, "The Upanishadas formulate philosophical conceptions unequalled in India or perhaps anywhere else in the world."[5]

Thus, the Indian culture is very rich. It is, therefore, surprising that Indians themselves should not be able to fully appreciate the worth of their own achievements. This can be, to an extent, attributed to centuries of foreign rule which tried to demolish the vestiges of India's culture. The absence of a culture base in education, which unfortunately continues even now, could be the other reason. Afterall, Macauley, on whose Minute, the foundation of India's modern system of education was laid, believed that a few shelves of English literature were sufficient to contain the totality of India's literature. Whereas a section of the population under the influence of foreign education moved away from its rich cultural values, the village folks and the women, who were somehow left out from the western and other foreign influences, adhered to the old cultural values and preserved them. Unfortunately, these people having been relegated to a subservient position, were preoccupied with the struggle for existence and did not have much power to contribute to cultural regeneration of the country. Through folklore and religious practices, however, they contributed to the preservation of culture and the values which are so characterstic of the Indian psyche.

Today, India's cultural heritage is mostly treasured in our ancient books, subsequent commentaries of scholars on this literature and with the village and the women folk. The government, has, in recent times, initiated steps to preserve the contributions that were made in the past. These include preservation of monuments, support of performing and plastic arts etc. A number of organisations are also now engaged in the work of dissemination of India's past cultural heritage as well as of its present achievement. It is for the educational institutions to carry forward this work with speed and in a big way.

References and Notes

1. *Report of the Education Commission* 1964-66, para 11.09 pp. 502-503.
2. *Programme of Action , National policy on Education 1986;* Government of India, Ministry of Human Resources Development; pp. 171-179.
3. Swami Ranganathananda, *Eternal Values for a Changing Society,* Bharatiya Vidya Bhavan, Bombay, 1971, p.8.
4. Bahadur Krishna P, *The Wisdom of Yoga, A Study of Patanjali's Yoga Sutra,* Sterling Publishers Private.
5. Ibid.

6

Anti Social Behaviour

Nature observes its laws meticulously. Being a product of nature, man should, logically speaking, follow the codes of behaviour laid down by society. However, this is not always so. It would, therefore, be interesting to study why man violates the social norms and takes to certain behaviour patterns which are sometimes harmful to him, sometimes to the group around him and at times to both.

Causes of Anti-social Behaviour

A statement was incorporated in the questionnaire to assess the relative importance of certain causes which are considered to be at the root of an individual's or a group's anti-social behaviour. The statement was worded as follows:

"Anti-social acts originate from the following causes —

(a) Financial hardships;

(b) Lack of education among those who commit such acts;

(c) Bad influence of mass media such as films, T.V.".

(G-15)

Respondents were requested to grade the above causes. Weighted-scores for the above causes are indicated below.

Grading Causes of Wrong Actions

Statement	No. of persons who allotted first, second and third position to this statement			No. of person, who expressed no opinion.	Weighted scores
	I–Position	II–Position	III–Position		
(a)	362	259	145	115	66.2%
(b)	292	269	206	114	61.3%
(c)	109	238	417	117	46.2%

Anti-social acts are of two kinds :

(a) Crimes where violence is used;

(b) Crimes, which largely require the application of one's grey matter rather than physical force.

With the spread of education and the development of human-brain, new types of crimes are emerging which require more of intelligence than force. As it is largely the white-collar class which is involved in these crimes, such crimes are known as white-collar crimes. Examples of such crimes are fabrication of fake university diplomas and degrees, immoral traffic, cheating, forgery, pilfering civic property, tax-evasion, distorted interpretation of rules and laws, smuggling, foreign exchange rackets, acceptance of kick-backs etc. etc.

There are many causes of the crimes. Of the three causes listed in the questionnaire, the respondents graded them in the descending order as given in the foregoing statement (G-15).

A study done in this connection regarding responsibility of the school for children's delinquency led to the following interesting and surprising results.

"After following a group of school children for eleven years, a team of researchers concluded that school relationships are the third most important contributors to delinquency, following only the family and the poor group."[1]

Another study by Delbert S. Eliot found the school itself and not the family or "the streets" to be critical for generation of delinquent behaviour.[2]

"Researchers have held that schools promote delinquency in the following way. Students who are unable to meet the expectations of their teachers are rejected by them. In this process of alteration, they become truant and rebellious and drift into association with the delinquent sub-culture. —Eliot and Voss, by following 2600 junior high school students for four years, found that delinquency rate was significantly lower among those who dropped out than it was among those with similar academic records who remained in school."[3]

Thus, the school teachers become responsible for delinquency of children in two ways :

(a) By alienating students by adopting an attitude of indifference to those who do not perform well in academics;

(b) By ignoring those who are drop-outs due to one reason or the other.

In other words, in terms of the studies quoted above, indifference to education comes to occupy very near, if not actually, the first position, among the list of causes for commiting crimes.

Bribes:

The following statement was included in the questionnaire for students to know their reaction to bribery, which is one of the white-collar crimes.

"It is pardonable, if a needy person accepted bribe". (S-3)

The following score-chart gives indication of the students views in this connection.

Permissiveness for Accepting Bribe

S.No.	Category. of respondents	Number agreeing	Number undecided	Number disagreeing	Number of persons who expressed no opinion
1.	Total students population	36	48	181	2
	(267)	(13.5)	(18)	(67.8)	(0.7)
2.	School students (M)	6	16	48	-
	(70)	(8.6)	(22.8)	(68.6)	
3.	School students (F)	10	17	59	-
	(86)	(11.6)	(19.8)	(68.6)	
4.	College students (M)	10	4	18	2
	(34)	(29.5)	(11.7)	(52.9)	(5.9)
5.	College students(F)	9	11	50	-
	(70)	(12.9)	(15.7)	(71.4)	-
6.	African students (M)	1	-	6	-
	(7)	(14.3)	-	(85.7)	-

As noticed above, comparatively the least opposition to the statement was from college-students (male). All other categories of students opposed the practice of acceptance of bribe to a greater extent even by a needy person. It can not be denied that indulging in bribes has greater bearing in one's attitude of mind than on one's needs. Once we fall a prey to this practice, the habit overtakes us and thereafter bribe is accepted not for meeting our needs, but to satisfy our lust for money. It is unfortunate that bribery has become rampant in India in recent decades.

An Indian politician once said, "If you strike a spade in Saudi Arabia, you well get oil, but if you do so in India, you will find corruption.[4] In these circumstances, if one condones bribery, existing moral chaos in the society is bound to worsen. Therefore, the evil is rightly punishable under the law.

Drinking :

The statement included in the questionnaire on this issue was as follows:

"Salamat and John were discussing drinking. Salamat argued that one should totally keep away from alcoholic drinks. John, on the other hand, felt that drinking to a limited degree to keep company should be acceptable to the society.

Who do you agree with ?

(a) Salamat, who totally rejects drinking

OR

(b) John who accepts drinking in moderation for company sake". (G-3)

Response-pattern to the above statement was as follows:

Abstinence Vs. Moderate Drinking

Option	No. of persons agreeing	No of persons dis-agreeing	No of persons un-decided or who expressed no opinion
(a)	542 (61.5)	5 (0.6)	25
OR			
(b)	307 (34.8)	2 (0.2)	(2.9)

Total number of respondents was 881. Thus there was an

above-average support for the option favouring total rejection of drinking.

While debating the above statement, one has to take into account several dimensions of this issue.

(a) What should be taken as norm of moderate drinking ?

(b) If drinking is to be allowed, what should be the minimum age of the person before he takes to drinking ?

When Mikhail Gorbachov came to power in the USSR in March 1985, in order to curb the drinking habit among the youth, he raised the drinking age in the country to 21 years.

(c) There may be certain areas in which drinking has come to be connected with one's work. For example, business parleys and diplomatic jobs are considered to be more conducive to initiate a person into drinking habit. If one is to talk of total abstinence, one also must take situations like these into account.

Though solitary or exceptional cases do not establish any rule, yet a concrete example here would provide a food for thought. A Minister of Information and Broadcasting in the Indian Union Cabinet in the seventies of this century did not drink. He was advised by his friends to start drinking, at least in moderation, otherwise, the journalist would not like to 'spoil their evenings' with him merely over a cup of tea. As incharge of Information and Broadcasting Ministry, the Ministers' frequent meetings with the journalists were highly essential. Notwithstanding the fact that he was keen on developing a proper equation with editors and correspondents of the newspapers as well as the writers' world, he did not take recourse to drinking, still the journalists and writers were his regular visitors, because he was highly intelligent and had enough to offer to them by way of news and have a purposeful dialogue with them on various political, economic and social issues. Later, when this very minister was appointed, in the cabinet rank, as ambassador to the USSR, even in his diplomatic assignment also he did not initiate himself into the drinking habit, yet he was highly successful in his mission. This example shows that in political and diplomatic jobs one can manage without drinking if one is properly equipped otherwise for the functions assigned to him or her.

Similarly in the business sphere, one can achieve the desired success by being resourceful and honest in his dealings. More-over, consuming a peg and offering one to a guest are two different things. If your work or the situation demands that you are to offer a glass of wine to a guest, it does not mean that you cannot get yourself excused from sharing the same.

(d) There are people, who hold that drinking is outside the domain of social morality and it is purely a personal matter. As such, drinking should have no social stigma attached to it. Is it an issue of personal freedom or that of personal eccentricity? It has to be seen in proper perspective and the social hazards that drinking poses have to be taken fully into account.

Further, it should be remembered that drinking is quite common among those persons also who later become drug-addicts or take to illegal distillation and illegal trading in spirits. Drug addiction and drug trading is assuming frightening dimensions in India. India was having more than one and a half crores of drug-addicts in the year 1988. Geographically, our country is quite vulnerable to drug smuggling and drug trading because countries located in the vicinity of India trade in narcotics. These countries are Nepal, Burma, Thailand, Pakistan and Afghanistan. Therefore, the question of drinking has to be viewed in this overall perspective and decided whether it constitutes or does not constitute a part of social morality.

The opposition to drinking is believed to be on the following grounds.

(i) "Alcohol (when taken in excess) depresses the activity of the central nervous system and thereby interferes with coordination, reaction time and reasoning ability. —The harmful effects of excessive drinking on the liver are well-known; the end result may be cirrhosis, a condition in which liver cells are destroyed by alcohol and replaced by scar tissues. —In addition to physical effects, alcohol contributes to several social problems.[5] These social problems include suicides, murders, sexual assaults, release of animal instinct in man, broken homes, financial problems and numerous other anti-social and unhealthy situations. According to an assessment by the Soviet Union, one third of crimes in that country were linked to drunkenness.[6]

* Innumerable tests of physical and mental performance show that alcohol reduces visual acuity and delays recovery from visual dazzle, impairs taste, smell and hearing, muscular coordination and steadiness, and prolongs reaction time. It leads to alcohol dependence.

*The effects of alcohol and psychotropic drugs on motor

---

* For detailed study, read Laurance D.R. and Bennet P.N.: *Clinical Pharmacology* (Sixth Edition): Churchil Livingstone (U.K.), 1987, pp 398-419.

driving have been intensively studied. There is impressive evidence to demonstrate that alcohol plays a huge part in causing motor accidents, being a factor perhaps in as many as 50%. It is revealed that alcohol brings disaster on the road less because of lack of skill than because of defective judgement in relation to skill. For this reason, compulsory roadside breath-test and provision for blood-test (if necessary) have been acknowledged to be in public interest. The two diagrams given at the end of this chapter* bring out features of alcohol dependence and its effects on driving.

One may say that the issue under consideration was a comparison between total abstinence and moderate drinking and not excessive drinking; but generally it so happens that once a person takes to drinking, in due course of time the limits of moderate and excessive drinking are obliterated. Social drinking (for companionship) can, many a time, result in regular drinking habit.

Those who approve of drinking in moderation advance some of the following arguments:

(a) Drinking is a symbol of modernity.

(b) Among Christians, drinking is an integral part of religious customs and of normal life, especially on festivities.

(c) It is argued, what is wrong if a soldier takes a peg or two of whisky while performing his duty on a snow-clad mountain post at a height of say about 15000 feet? Similarly, there is nothig wrong if a washer-man, who has to do his work in India by standing in pond or river-water for hours together even on chilly winter-mornings, to consume a peg or two of a drink.

(d) It is believed that an occasional peg of whisky contributes to the efficient working of the heart. Proponents of this view possibly ignore the effect of alcohol on the liver.

It would be pertinent to allude to the reaction of the respondents belonging to the medical profession on the statement (G-3) pertaining to drinking.

Response-Pattern

Option	No of persons agreeing	No of persons dis-agreeing	No of persons who did not express any opinion or were undecided.
(a)	8 (40)	-	1
OR			
(b)	10+1 (50+5)	-	5

Thus 55 per cent of the medical practitioners were ready to tolerate drinking in moderation*.

Figures of registered drug addicts, as revealed by the Secretary General of the Association for Social Health in India, New Delhi, indicate that 39% of them started taking drugs for curiosity sake only and 35% when they were compelled to do so in the company of their friends. If these figures are any guide in respect of drinking also, there is hardly room for any doubt that moderation in drinking and social drinking can later lead to regular drinking and even to addiction.

The following beer consumption statistics make a useful reading.

World Beer Consumption per Person over the Age of 15 Years[7]

S.No.	Region of the World	Consumption 1960	Consumption 1981	Increase per cent
1	2	3	4	5
1.	Central and Western African countries	8.2 ltres	61.1 ltrs.	52.9 ltrs OR 64.5%
2.	North America	84.5 ltrs.	120.7 ltrs.	36.2 ltrs. OR 43%
3.	Countries of South America	20.5 ltrs.	46.4 ltrs.	25.9 ltrs. OR 126%

* Note : Among the medical practitioner there was onlty one female and she agreed with part(b) of the statement.

1	2	3	4	5
4.	Countries of Central America and the Caribbean	12.1 ltrs.	35.7 ltrs	23.6 ltrs OR 195 %
5.	Countries of East Asia.	3.7 ltrs	24.4 ltrs	20.7 OR 560%

These statistics lead to the following conclusions:

(a) The industrialised countries outdrink the developing countries.

(b) The percentage increase in the consumption of beer in the underdeveloped and developing countries is however, much more than in the developed countries.

If drinking habit is to be curbed or to be kept under control, people must be educated on the harmful effects of drinking. In this regard, light may have to be thrown on some of the following aspects in the educational institutions.

(i) Addiction — a drag on economy and a social evil.

(ii) Falseness of the notion that drinking relieves a person of his frustrations and tensions.

(iii) Drinking as a factor for inducing sleep or sleeplessness.

(iv) Effect of drinking on appetite.

(v) Effect of drinking on various organs of the body, including nervous system, brain, human hearing system, eyesight, sense of smell etc.

(vi) Diseases caused as a result of drinking.

Besides, facilities for the availability of alcoholic drinks may be reduced by decreasing the number of working days of the stores selling drinks, reducing their working hours, cutting down the production of alcoholic beverages etc. Alcoholic drinks may have to be made costlier. But great-foresight and caution will have to be exercised while introducing these or other similar measures so that in the process of imposing curbs illicit practices are not encouraged.

Smoking:

The statement on this subject is below:

Mahesh and Rakesh were exchanging views on smoking. Mahesh said that one should never smoke. Rakesh said that limited smoking for the sake of keeping company should not be looked down upon. Who in your opinion is right ?

(a) Mahesh, who totally opposes smoking

OR

(b) Rakesh, who favours smoking within limits for the sake of company." (S-2)

The opinion-chart on this statement indicated as follows:

Non-smoking Vs. Smoking within limits

Option	No. of persons agreeing	No. of persons disagreeing	No. of persons who expressed no opinion or were undecided
(a)	200	5	6
	(74.9)	(2.2)	
OR			
(b)	54	2	
	(20.2)	(0.8)	(2.2)

Thus there was a high score in support of the statement suggesting total opposition to smoking.

Composition of Tobacco Smoke

The composition of tobacco smoke is complex (about 500 compounds have been identified in it) and varies with the type of tobacco and the way it is smoked. The chief pharmacologically active ingredients are nicotine (acute effects) and tars (chronic effects).

Smoke of cigars and pipes is alkaline (p^H 8.5) and nicotine is relatively un-ionized and lipid soluble so that it is readily absorbed in the mouth. Cigar and pipe smokers thus obtain nicotine without inhaling (they also have a lower death rate from lung cancer).

Smoke of cigarettes is acidic (p^H 5.3) and nicotine is relatively ionized and insoluble in lipids. Desired amounts of nicotine are only absorbed if it is taken into the lungs, where the enormous surface area for absorption compensates for the relative lipid insolubility. Cigarette smokers therefore inhale (they have a high rate of death from lung cancer). The amount of nicotine absorbed from tobacco smoke varies from 90% in those who inhale to 10% in those who do not.

Tobacco smoke contains 1-5% carbon monoxide and habitual smokers have 3-7% (heavy smokers as much as 15%) of their haemoglobin as carboxy-haemoglobin, which cannot carry oxygen. This is sufficient to reduce exercise capacity in patients with angina pectoris."

Dangers of Smoking:

One of the harmful constituents of tobacco is nicotine. This element has been named after the French diplomat J. Nicot, who introduced tobacco into France in 1860. Nicotine is the poisonous alkaloid extracted from tobacco as oily liquid.[8] According to one observation, "If nicotine of two cigarettes in pure form is injected into the system of a human-being, he would die in a short while, as he would take when hit by a gun bullet."

Some people regard tobacco more harmful than liquor, one of the important reasons for this being that a smoker goes on consuming nicotine during most part of his waking hours. Other harmful effects of tobacco which students need to be apprised of are as follows. Tobacco is harmful for every part of the body. It reduces one's age. "The time by which a habitual smokers' life is shortened is about 5 min per cigarette smoked." Dolland and his colleagues in 1951 sent a questionnaire on smoking habits to all British doctors. Their respondents' evaluation, after 20 years of 34440 smokers, revealed as follows:

1) Of these 10072 had died.
2) Death rate of cigarette smokers was twice that of life-long non-smokers.
3) Smoking caused death chiefly by :

   a. —heart-disease;
   b. —lungs cancer;
   c. —chronic obstructive lung disease;
   d. —various vescular diseases.

Lungs cancer accounted for 37,000 deaths in U.K. in 1974. Medical opinion indicates that if coal-tar content in cigarettes is reduced, deaths from lung cancer would fall by 80% within 20 years.

The risk of smokers developing mouth and throat cancers is 5-10 times greater than that for non-smokers. It is as great for pipe and cigar smokers as for cigarette smokers. Cancers of pancreas, kidney and urinary tract are also commoner in smokers.

A smoker has ten fold chances of contracting a heart disease as compared to a non-smoker. If nicotine is consumed by ladies who use contraceptives also, their chance of heart-disease multiplies further. According to one opinion, tobacco smoke contains 2000 harmful elements. Smoking leads to cancer of the larynx, mouth, and oesophagus as well as to lung-cancer. Bronchitis, emphysema, ulcers as well as circulatory diseases are related to smoking, not to speak of many fires which are caused due to smokers' carelessness. By consuming one packet of cigarettes every day, the smoker accumulates 840 cubic centimetres of coal tar in the system by the end of a year.

*Among the causes leading to coronary heart disease (CHD), the most important were cholesterol in the blood, high blood pressure and cigarette smoking. Under the age of 65, smokers are about twice as likely to die of CHD as are non-smokers and heavy smokers about 3½ a times as likely.

The obstructive syndrome is as specifically related to smoking as is being cancer and poses relatively more risks to life than even lung cancer.

In view of the above, laws make it incumbent on the manufacturers of cigarettes to display a warning on the cigarette packs that the product is injurious to health. Canada has perhaps the most stringent laws in the world on tobacco advertisements. Certain contraventions of this law carry a penalty upto 300,000 Candian dollars.

Forms of Tobacco Consumption

There are various forms in which tobacco may be consumed by a person.

(a) *Sniffing*: Powdered, fermented and scented preparation of tobacco is taken by inhaling. This may contribute to nasal cancer.

(b) *Chewing tobacco*: It is more conveniet than smoking a pipe, cigar or a cigarette as no lighting is required in this case. It exposes one to the risk of mouth cancer.

(c) *Cigarette smoking*: Tobacco is rolled inside a piece of paper, which is pasted and thereafter cut into requisite sizes. The spread of the practice of sniffing tobacco in the west is attributed to the 18th century, that of tobacco chewing to the 19th century, of cigarette-smoking to the 20th century, particularly to the 1920's — the period following the world war-I. According to the Encyclopedia Britannica,

"In the 20th century, statistics showed that the practice of smoking continued to increase, particularly among women and young people".[9]

(d) *Pipe Smoking*

According to the Encyclopedia Britannica, "The smoking of tobacco through pipe is indigenous to the Americas and derives from the religious ceremonies of ancient priests in Mexico. Farther north, American Indians developed ceremonial pipes — the chief of these being calumet or pipe for peace. Such pipes had marble or red steatite (for pipestone) bowls and ash stems about 30 to 40 inches long and were decorated with hair and feathers. The practice of pipe smoking reached Europe through sailors who had encountered it in the New World."[10]

In the Indian rural situation, at times, a young one is initiated into smoking when he is repeatedly asked to prepare 'hukka' for his parents and grandparents and inhale it too in order to ensure that the tobacco in contact with ambers is ready for inhaling.

According to Laurance and Bennet, one-third of regular smokers began smoking before they were nine. The earlier in life a person starts smoking, the greater is the risk to his health and the life span. If parents smoke, their children are liable to follow their example. Smoking is found to be less common in schools where teachers are non-smokers. If a person reaches 20 without smoking, he is less likely to take to this habit thereafter.

Sigmund Freud was a life-long tobacco addict. He suggested that some children may be victims of a constitutional intensification of the erotogenic significance of the labial region, which, if it persists, will provide a powerful motive for smoking.

Mold's Discovery

About two decades ago, Dr. James Mold, an employee of a cigarette manufacturing company in America, discovered a catalyst which he claimed could protect the smokers from contracting cancer. He said, "we are ecstatic over the fact that we had done something that no one in the world had been able to do."

However, the company's legal adviser counselled his clients not to market the product, otherwise they would be sued for selling something which they themselves have now proved was injurious to public health and they may have to pay compensation for it. So the company shelved the proposal. "God alone knows, how many cancer cases (were) promoted and 'murders committed' by not implementing Dr. Mold's discovery," writes Khuswant Singh.[11]

Measures to Curb Smoking

(1) Educating the public through educational institutions, mass-media, voluntary agencies and particularly through associations of medical experts on the harmful effects of smoking will be an effective measure in this regard. These media can play a useful role in weaning the people away from smoking.

(2) Students may be apprised of the damage that nicotine, consumed in various forms, can cause to the human-system. Tranquillisers, drugs, acupuncture, nicotine chewing-gums etc. are not very effective aids to wean people from smoking. A strong will to stop smoking and long course of education on the harmful effects of smoking are the best aids to decrease the incidence of smoking. They should be told that there is no virtue in smoking for company's sake as there is none in committing suicide for company's sake.

(3) Smoking should be banned in all closed public places such as offices, buses, underground railway stations, cinema halls, restaurants etc., as has been done in the USSR. In some cities of India, smoking is banned in buses owned by the government; but this ban is observed more in breach than in observance. It would be appropriate to mention here an Australian episode; "A bus driver, Carroll, 59, an employee of the Melbourne Transit Authority, sued the authority for a compensation as he had contracted cancer due to his exposure to passive smoking on account of smoking by passengers in the bus, though smoking was banned in public transport in 1976. The court awarded a compensation of 52,000 Australian dollars to the Victim.[12]

(4) The far-reaching effects of passive smoking should also be publicised among the people. Not many people are aware of the fact that they are liable to suffer from the harmful effects resulting from active smoking if they keep close company with the smokers, notwithstanding that they may be non-smokers.

(5) The students and the general public should be told about the extent of paper which cigarette wrappings consume. This, in turn leads to depletion of forests and importing of more paper from abroad against foreign exchange.

(6) The cigarette manufacturers should be banned, by law, to

use the name of gods or eminent persons as their trade-mark such as Ganesh Bidi.

Sex Indulgence

Sex is the basis of all life. The different mythological theories of creation write about various sexual acts such as of the sky and the earth. It is held that Eros (i.e., sexual love) or 'Kama' was one of the first creations of the universal egg from which all creation followed, though Adam is believed to have been expelled from Heaven on account of not having been able to control his sex instinct. Kama (sexual instinct) has been described in the ancient Vedas and the subsequent works as all pervading and invincible. It is present in human beings, animals, birds, creepers, trees, fruits, flowers and, in short, in all life forms. During the period of youth, its impulse tends to become irresistible.

Matrimony is essential for the evolution of life. Numerous sages and great personalities tasted the joys of married life. If they did not, how would it be possible to propagate and perpetuate the genes of good people in this world! In Indian history, there is a mention of so many *risis* having led a married life before becoming ascetics. All this shows that sex instinct and the urge to multiply is natural and universal in all humans.

Pre-Marital Sex

Post-marital sex being a normal phenomenon of life, a statement to study the attitude of the society only to pre-marital sex was included in the questionnaire. As pre-marital sex indulgence concerns the unmarried persons only, this statement was included in the questionnaire for students. This statement was as follows.

> "No stigma should be attached to sexual relations before marriage". (S-9)

The reaction of the respondents is given below:

Pre-marital Sex Indulgence

S.No	Category	No. agreeing	No. undecided	No. disagreeing
1	2	3	4	5
(1)	Total population (267)	58 (21.7)	27 (10.1)	182 (68.2)
(2)	School students (M) (70)	14 (20)	14 (20)	42 (60)

1	2	3	4	5
(3)	School students (F) (86)	8 (9.3)	9 (10.5)	69 (80.2)
(4)	College students (M) (34)	20 (34)	1 (2.9)	13 (38.2)
(5)	College students (F) (70)	12 (17.1)	3 (4.3)	55 (78.6)
(6)	African students (7)	4 (57.1)	-	3 (42.9)

The preceding table indicates that college students approve of the idea of pre-marital sex to a higher degree than their counterparts in schools. This may be attributed, to an extent, to the demand of the age. Girls seem to be opposing the suggestion of pre-marital sex much more than the boys, including those who are in college. One of the reasons for this could be that the girls realise that the stakes involved for them in pre-marital sex relationship are far greater than those for boys. Pre-marital sex relationship especially if it results in pregnancy, can ruin the subsequent married and family life of the girl or even the chance of marriage itself. It is interesting to note that in a tradition-bound society, which taboos pre-marital sex, a large proportion of youths seem to be favouring it.

Pre-marital sex relationship may be of three kinds:

(a) When both partners are un-married.
(b) When one of the partners is married.
(c) Homosexual indulgence.

Views differ widely on this statement.

According to Waltermarck, "Among many uncivilised peoples, both sexes enjoy perfect freedom previous to marriage, and in some cases it is considered almost dishonourable for a girl to have no lover.—

The East African Barea and Kunama do not regard it as in the least disreputable for a girl to become pregnant nor do they punish nor censure the seducer. (Among the Wanyoro) it constantly happens that young girls spend the night with their lovers, only returning to their father's house in the morning, and this is not considered scandalous. (In Solomon Islands), female chastity is a virtue that would sound strange in the ear of the native. ...."[13] Among the Angami negros, men are desirous before marriage to have a proof that their wives will not be barren —Chastity begins with marriage.[14]

"In some cultures, (pre-marital sexual) intercourse is believed to be necessary if pre-adolescents are to mature sexually. The Trukese of Caroline Islands build small huts especially for this purpose. Among the Alorese of Indonesia, mothers routinely masturbate their children in order to pacify them."[15]

About half a century ago, Kinsey studied sex before marriage in America. His interviews between 1940-48, with some volunteers who agreed to cooperate with him in his study, included members of the social club as well as persons in prison (who of course can not be regarded as a true sample of the general society), revealed 85 per cent of all Americans had experienced premarital sex, 70 per cent had visited a prostitute and over one-third had participated in at least one homosexual act. Kinsey's data suggest that a wave of sexual liberation occurred much earlier than is usually believed, probably in the generation that came of age after world war-I. His study found that only 8 per cent of white women born before 1900 had premarital intercourse before the age of 20, but that among those born between 1910 and 1929 the figure was 22 per cent. Later surveys indicate that the second wave of liberation occurred in the second half of the 1960s and the early 1970s. Kinsey found that two-thirds of the single women aged 18 to 25 in his sample were virgins, while Hunt's survey, conducted in the 1970s, found that only one-fourth of the single women in this age bracket were virgins."[16]

Among Muslims

Shi 'ite school in Islam believes in Mut 'ah, which is defined as a fixed-term marriage before the regualr matrimonial alliance. Its main features are as follows:

(a) A man and a woman may enter into a matrimonial contract for a fixed period, which may or may not be renewed. It may lead to a regular marriage as well.

(b) In this temporary kind of marriage, man has no obligation to pay the expenses of the woman as in the case of a regular marriage.

(c) In a regular marriage, woman is to accept man as the head of the family; but in the case of Mut 'ah, she may not accept him as the head of the household.

(d) Any of the two partners can exercise birth-control

without the consent of the other. In Islam, birth control is permitted before conception takes place; but abortion is not allowed in Islam.

This custom of legalised pre-marital sex has both pros and cons.

Pros

By the time a girl or a boy reaches 18 years of age, sex instinct develops in the individual; but social maturity and financial independence is yet to come about. Therefore, regular marriage cannot be recommended in such circumstances. On the contrary, ceilbacy can also create psychological and emotional problems. Therefore, to avert chances of 'sexual communism', in which case any boy can mate with any girl, Mut 'ah is recommended which puts some limits on the pre-marital relations.

Cons

The opponents of Mut 'ah argue that this system amounts to licensing and codifying sex-experience prior to marriage. Further, sex indulgence is a chain-reaction, and depending on the opportunities available, young boys and girls can become victims of promiscuity. Whereas Mut 'ah may satisfy animal instincts in a man or a woman, it militates against mutual loyalty.

Chastity

Contrary to this, chastity is prized as a great virtue by many societies. Hindu ethics as well as that of the Christians lay emphasis on self-mortification and ascetism, whereas Islam refuses to accept that sex-abstinence is a necessary constituent of high morals. Speaking before a rally of 400,000 young people in Satiago DE Compostela on August 20, 1989, Pope John Paul warned the youths against the dangers of easy sex, saying that a materialist society had robbed love of its real content. He added that modern ways of life had reduced "love to a temporary experience of personal gratification and even of mere sexual enjoyment.— How can you not recognise in all this the worm of a consumist mentality which has slowly emptied love of its transcendent content?" (The Statesman, New Delhi, 21-8-89, p.8)

Among the Moroura tribe in Australia and in Nias, sexual intercourse before marriage is punishable with death. Even among the Muslims, according to the religious laws rape before or after marriage is punishable with death.

Among several civilised nations, different standards of sex-morality are applied to men and women. Chastity is considered a male virtue and a female duty, which obviously, amounts to having double standards in sex matters.

In the balance, one may be inclined to think that the temporary marriage recommended in Islam would be better than the irresponsible sex-indulgence or what is sometimes termed as communism in sex and also better than cohabitation with prostitutes or members of the same sex; but this is not all. It has several negative factors also. Man always desires to marry a virgin. Even the college students who, expressed no objection to sex before marriage would not be inclined to marry a non-virgin girl. The off-springs of unmarried mothers are a social problem. Also, it hurts the life of a child who is born as a result of pre-marriage intercourse. if in the pre-marital sex experience one of the partners is married, it becomes a case of conjugal infidelilty. In this case also, if the woman becomes pregnant, the problem of illegitimate child becomes equally grave.

Teen-age Pregnancy

When we talk of pre-marital sex, we should be consicious of the gravity of teen-age pregnancy. An article appearing in the World Health Journal (April-June, 1988) on Teen-age Pregnancy in the America by CESAR A. Chelala (pages 22-23) is revealing. The writer calls it a new epidemic of modern times. "In Latin America as a whole, more than 20% of pregnancies occur in women below 18 years of age. In the Caribbean, almost 50% of all teenage births occur to women of 17 years old or younger. In the United States, close to one million adolescents between 15-19 years and 30,000 girls below 15 become pregnant every year. True estimates of pregnancy are lacking because at least 20% of pregnancies end in abortion, which is illegal throughout the region (except Cuba & U.S.A.). The early and great frequency of sexual activity among teenagers seems to be a critical factor. Many girls become pregnant because they are ignorant about the basics of the sex act or the birth control. ".......a U.S. national survey estimated that almost 70% of premarital pregnancies among teenagers were unwanted". " One U.S. study among 180 pregnant students found a prevalance of attempted suicides of 13 per cent".

Pregnancies are likely to be more in the case of girls in lower socio-economic groups where both parents are working and do not have enough time to spend with their children.

Adolescent pregnancy has physical and psychological consequencies — lack of proper medical care, high child/mother mortality rate, more still-births, clandestine abortions risking lives, education getting hampered.

"The teen-age pregnancy rate in India varies between 8 to 14 per cent. ...... The Wardha study of 1000 pregnant teen-agers, who came for abortion, noted that 88 per cent of the girls had no knowledge of the possible consequences of sexual intercourse."[17]

With the increase in the population of youth and the family-planning programmes being regularly advertised all over, the curiosity of the youth to get acquainted with sex matters gets accentuated. If the youth are not given, the information which they desire to seek in this regard, they would try to secure information on this subject through channels which may be unreliable and misleading. It, therefore, appears essential to disseminate an authentic information on sex matters to the youth through informed channels.

Imparting Sex Education

In regard to sex education through schools and colleges, there was one statement in the questionnaire for students and one in the questionnaire for general non-student population. These statements are reproduced below:

" Sex education should be imparted in —
a) Schools;
b) Colleges." (S-12)

"Introduction of sex education would be desirable —
a) In colleges as well as schools
OR
b) In colleges only
OR
c) Neither in schools, nor in colleges" (G-12)

Students' response to the above statements is indicated in the following charts.

Imparting Sex Education: (S-12)

S.No.	Category	Statement	Number Agreeing	Number Undecided	Number Disagreeing	Number of persons who expressed no opinion
(1)	Total student population (267)	12(a)	157 (58.8)	49 (18.4)	60 (22.5)	1 (0.3)
(2)	Total student population (267)	12 (b)	166 (62.2)	77 (28.9)	18 (6.7)	6 (0 2)

Imparting Sex Education (G-12)

S.No.	Category	Statement	No. Agreeing	No. Undecided	No. Disagreeing
1.	Total population in general non-students category (881)	(a)	419 (47.6)		4
		OR		21	
		(b)	303 (34.3)	(2.4)	1
		OR			
		(c)	133 (15.1)		

In the case of the general population, only 15.1 per cent of the respondents felt that sex education should neither be imparted in schools nor in colleges; the rest were in favour of introduction of sex education in the educational system at some stage. As regards students, larger number of them favoured sex education at the college stage. Surprisingly, the college students (M) did not support this idea to the extent the college students (F) did. Further comparison between the extent of agreement expressed by school and college students in case of statement (S-12) of the questionnaire brings out the following picture:

Comparative Study of the Opinions Expressed by School and College Students: (S-12)

S.No.	Category	Statement	Extent of agreement	Statement	Extent of agreement
1	2	3	4	5	6
1.	School students (M) (70)	12(a)	38 (54.3)	12(b)	37 (52.9)
2.	School students (F) (86)	-do-	36(51.8)	-do-	48 (55.8)
3.	College students (M) (34)	-do-	27(79.4)	-do-	23(67.6)

1	2	3	4	5	6
4.	**College students (F) (70)**	**12(a)**	**49 (70)**	**12(b)**	**53 (75.8)**
5.	**African College students (M) (7)**	**-do-**	**7(100)**	**-do-**	**5(71.4)**

While imparting sex education, one has to have due regard to the age-level of the students and their total environments. The students in cities, possibly, have a greater need for sex education than their counterparts in villages whose exposure to the exhibition of sexy situations is less. This happens because the invasion of western culture, sex-stimulating films and advertisements is more on the inhabitants of the cities than those living in villages.

Role of Mass-Media

In any educational programme, mass media have an important role to play. Therefore, while considering the type of educational programmes on sex-education, it may have to be examined how far some of the pictures exhibited on the silver screen and the material appearing in the print media would help or hinder the desirable sex-education process. The statement pertaining to this aspect, as given in the questionnaire for the general population, was as follows:

> "There is not much harm in exhibiting pictures with sex-appeal in newspapers, on T.V. and cinema screen" (G-4)

Out of the 881 respondents, only 16.6 per cent agreed with this statement, whereas 695 of them (i.e., 78.9 per cent) disagreed and 4.5 per cent of them were undecided. Though the wording of this statement had the following flaws, yet the high percentage of 78.9 per cent makes the verdict of the respondents very clear. These flaws are:

(a) the use of 'not much' make the statement somewhat elusive;

(b) the term 'sex-appeal' is used in good sense also, though in this case its import and the Hindi translation of the statement made it clear that 'sex appeal' in this context meant 'sex-stimulating situation'.

Curriculum

The curriculum for sex-education could be drawn up on the following lines :

a) **Pre-school stage—Home Education**

(1) At the pre-school early stages, the child desires to know how he came into this world. He also derives some pleasure in play with his genitalia.

It is for the parents and not the school to tell the child that he came out of the mother's tummy. Mother can also show some animals or women who are pregnant to make her explanations simpler. As regards playing with genitals, the education has to be practical i.e., by covering the child's organs with napkins or panties so that the child does not develop this practice.

(b) **School and College Curricula**

Education at the school and subsequent stage may include the following information:

(2) Development of egg cells in the body among animals which do not lay egg.

(3) Emotional ties between young ones and the family in humans as well as animals.

(4) Secretion of sex harmones and their effect, menstruation cycles in girls, wearing of sanitary pads, pain during menstruation and other allied problems and their precautions, pregnancy, semen formation in boys,and wet dreams.

(5) Causes of artificial sex stimulation —such as obscene literature, excess consumption of tea, tobacco, coffee and spicy foods.

(6) Masturbation and its harmful effects.

(7) (Near adulthood) Coitus act resulting in pregnancy, danger to life, illegitimate children, abortion, contraceptions, promiscuity, prostitution, venereal diseases.

(8) Homosexuality and its harmful effects. Harmful results of pre-marital sex, need for sex-abstinence, effect of extra-martial sex on the harmony of family life.

(9) Causes and Consequences of 'Aides'.

Sex education can be imparted more easily through subjects like physiology, biology, nature-study etc. Sex education should also include the question of sex ethics and advice on a balanced, responsible and happy family life.[18] With the weakening of the family ties after the break-up of the joint family system, particularly in the urban area, the need for 'family education' has tremendously increased. Some of the Indian temple architecture, like that of the

Konark Temple in Orissa, and stone sculptures and paintings elsewhere can provide a very good material for education on this erotic subject in a sublime manner.

Some people feel that sex is instinctive and no education is necessary in matters of sex. Such persons, perhaps, take a limited perspective of sex-education. There is much more in sex than sex alone— the aesthetics, the dedication and so on. Therefore, instruction in sex matters is essential. As any discussion on sex has been treated in the Indian society, for centuries now, as an area of secrecy, the teachers charged with the responsibility of imparting sex education will have to be given a thorough training in this subject, both in content and pedagogy, so that they can debate various issues pertaining to sex in a normal way and with natural ease and without getting embarrassed in any manner.

References and Notes

1. Feldhusen J. Thurston J. Benning J; *A Longitudinal Study of Delinquency and Other Aspects of Children's Behaviour*; International Journal of Criminology and Penology 1, 1973, p. 341-351.
2. Eliot Delbert S and Voss Harwin L; *Delinquency and Drop Out*, Lexington, Mass; Lexington Books; 1974 p. 204.

   also reproduced in

   Coleman James and Crossey Donald; *Social Problems;* Harper and Row, New York, 1984; p. 114.
3. Ibid, pages 121 and 206.
4. Dev Dutt; (art.) *Corruption in India;* The Hindustan Times, New Delhi, August 22, 1988.
5. Coleman James and Cressey Donald; *Social Problems;* Harper and Row, New York, 1984; p. 367.
6. The Hindustan Times, Evening News, June 14, 1988, p.1.
7. WHO's World Health Statistical Annual, 1987 quoted in World Health Journal, April, 1988.
8. The Concise Oxford Dictionary.
9. Encyclopedia Britannica, Vol. 3, 1988; p. 319.
10. Ibid, Vol. 9, p. 459.
11. Khushwant Singh, (art) *Murder for Money,* The Hindustan Times, New Delhi, July 23, 1988; p. 11.
12. The Hindustan Times, New Delhi, July 23, 1988; p. 12.
13. Watermarck Edward; *The Origin and Development of Moral Ideas,* Vol. II; Macmillan and Co. Ltd., London, 1924; p. 422.
14. Ibid, p. 423.
15. Coleman James and Cressey Donald; *Social problems,* Second Edition; Harper and Row, New York, 1984, p. 312.

16. Ibid, p. 312.
17. The Times of India, New Delhi, March 8, 1989; p. 8.
18. For Syllabus of Sex Education See Mathur W; Sex Education—How and Why ? Association of Social Health in India, New Delhi, 1976; pp. 95-105.

7

Search for Priorities

Historically speaking, systematic search for ethical ideals in India begins with the advent of the Aryans. As one goes through the vedic literature such as the Mantras, the Brahmanas, the aranyakas, the Upanisads and the post-vedic literature, one finds a continuous evolution of ideals. Crawford remarks that the Indian ethical ideals of the vedic period travel from objective level to subjective level culminating on the super-ethical level.[1] He says that in its objective aspect, the Hindu Dharma is tridimensional —Asramadharma, Varnadharma and Sadharandharma. In its subjective aspect, it emphasises the importance of internal sanctions for values whereas at the super-ethical level, it is a search for the Cosmic Energy.

The Tridemensional Code

Asramadharma provides for the total needs of man as he passes through different chronological stage of life. These needs are listed as the four pursharthas' of equal importance, namely, dharma, artha, kama and moksa. Dharma is virtuous thought and action; Artha is economic well-being; Kama is fulfilment of desires; and Moksa is total liberation. Dharma, though a code of righteous conduct, attempts to bring about harmony in the actions of the individual as well as of the society. It does not undermine individual's economic prosperity or the fulfilment of desires as long as these do not militate against broader interest of the society. In this context Manu lays down:

"परित्येजेदर्थकामौ यौ स्यातां धर्मवर्जितौ ।
धर्म चाण्यसुखोदर्क लोकविक्रुष्टपेव च ।।[2]

i.e. wealth and happiness which are repugnant to righteousness must be discarded.

Artha (wealth) was given an important place in the ancient Indian ideals. Earning of wealth was never rejected as being of inferior value. Many teachers of the Upanisads were property-holders. Yajnavalkya, the most renowned among them, renounced the world and its riches, after he had fully enjoyed the domestic bliss in the company of his two wives.

Kama, i.e., craving for sex and other-wordly things, has been considered quite natural throughout in the Indian literature and there are numerous references to sex in the Vedic and the post-Vedic art and literature.

Varnadharma was basically meant to assign functions to individuals in accordance with their physical emotional, intellectual and spiritual frame. It attempted to give intellectuals and educators; defence personnel and administrators; traders and labourers to the society. It gave the society a kind of modern guilds. Unfortunately, later on it degenerated into 3000 odd castes and subcastes. It was possible for a Satyakama to be received as a disciple by Gautama in Upanisadic period; but when rigidities gripped the Varnadharma, no Satyakama was allowed to cross the Rubicon.[3]

Sadharanadharma included duties expected to be fulfilled by an individual irrespective of one's station in life i.e., varna or asrama. These were a kind of universal duties. Manu listed ten such duties. These are:

"धृति क्षमा दमोऽस्तेयं शौचमिन्द्रियनिग्रहः ।
धीर्विद्या सत्यंक्रोधो दशकं धर्मलक्षमणम् ।।"

i.e. steadfastness, forgiveness, application in dharma, nonstealing, cleanliness, control of senses, wisdom, learning, truthfulness and restraint of anger.[4]

Sri Sathya Sai Baba writes, "While defining human values, you may enumerate sixty different points. But, all the sixty are included in these six; compassion, fear of evil, forebearance, serenity, patience and non attachment.[5]

In fact the list of 84 values[6] which was appended to the questionnaire, can be, more or less, termed as a list of sadharanadharma. The respondents were required to mark five important values, in order of priority, — for the school stage and five important values for the college stage from this list. Many respondents found this list[7] too long. Some of them were of the view that it would have been better if only a few important values had been selected from this for the questionnaire. The 'Chart showing the number of sub-groups preferring different values' given in this chapter would reveal the risk involved for any investigator to undertake such a work on behalf of the respondents.

Analysis of the 84 Values Listed in the Appendix to the Questionnaire

The Appendix contains a list of 84 values, out of which the value of 'Simple Living' (at Serial numbers 58 and 76) had been listed twice. Because of this ambiguity, and keeping in view that some respondents may have picked it up at both these serial numbers, this value has not been taken into account for discussion. Therefore, the paragraphs that follow contain an account of 82 values only. Even otherwise also, this value was not considered important by the respondents of any of the Sub-Groups of the General population consisting of 881 persons.

2. Methodology Adopted For Analysis

(i) All the respondents for the purposes of this purpose were divided into two main groups, namely the General Population Group and the Student Group. The former group consisting of 881 respondents, was further divided into eleven sub-groups and the latter, consisting of 267 respondents, into four sub-groups. It is in this light that the terms 'Group' and 'Sub-Groups' are to be read in the discussion that follows. The name of various sub-groups are given below :

Sub-groups of the General Population 1	Number of Respondents in each sub-group 2	
1. General Population (Female)	103	General population refers to persons belonging to vocations other than the ones listed from serial Nos. 4 to 11 below.
2. General Population (Male)	312	
3. General Population (Rural-Male and Female)	84	Males: 72, Females: 12.
4. Defence personnel	26	
5. Medical Practitioners (Doctors) and Advocates.	37	Includes 10 Advocates See Appendix VIII.
6. Primary School Teachers (Male and Female)	49	Male Teachers: 11 See Appendix VIII.
7. Secondary School Teachers (Female)	69	
8. Secondary School Teachers (Male)	84	
9. College Teachers (Female)	39	

1		2
10. College Teachers (Male)	50	
11. Educationists	28	Includes Educational Planners, Educational Administrators and Heads of institutions also.

Sub-groups of the student population	Number of Respondents in each sub-groups
1. Male School Students	70*
2. Female School Students	86
3. Male College Students	41**
4. Female College Students	70

Note : * In order to ensure mature reactions, in the questionnaire was circulated to the Students of class/grade XII only.

** Seven male students from Africa, studying in the colleges of Delhi, have been clubbed with this group.

(ii) Wherever a sub-group had less than 25 members, its members were clubbed with its nearest homogeneous sub-group.

(iii) It was assumed that a sub-group considered a value important only if at least 10% of its members selected this value for being emphasised at the school and the college stage.

(iv) In order to study the inter-se difference in perception between the two main groups, namely those of the General Population and the Student Population, and intra-se polarisation of opinion between various Sub-Groups in regard to various Value-Statements, standardised value of the difference in the observed proportions, namely Z, was calculated. Whenever Z was greater than 3, it was concluded that the polarisation of opinions was a marked one. On the contrary, where Z was less than 3, it was inferred that the difference in the perceptions was due to chance only. In the latter case the P P value i.e., percentage of respondents or the proportion in the population favouring the Statement was taken as the deciding factor of the opinion of the Group for or against the Statement.

(v) The usual practice is to take the Z value of 2 as strong enough envidence (at the 5 per cent level of significance, in the statistical terminology). However, we have chosen a higher critical value of 3 instead of 2, (which corresponds to a much higher level (of 0.27 per cent) i.e., if really the sub-groups do not differ in their percentage of favourable responses, the chances of getting value of z larger in numerical value (i.e., less than -3.0 or greater than +3.0) is as low as only about 3 in 1000. The reason for taking this higher value as the threshold value is that we are examining for the difference in proportions only for items which have atleast one sub-group with a percentage of 10% or more. Thus in the items selected for scrutiny, bias in favour of larger proportions is introduced. Hence, to be on the safe side, this higher critical value is adopted while deciding whether different sub-groups can be thought of as being homogeneous in their perception of the value concerned or whether there is a perceptible difference in the proportion of individuals perceiving the item as important.

(vi) It may happen that for some values, some sub-groups have proportions greater than 10% while others have less than 10%. In that case, the z value indicates whether individual sub-groups should be treated as having different percentages (this is the case when z value for the item is less than 3) or whether whatever differences seen in the perception of sub-groups are to be attributed only to chance (this is the case when z value for the item is smaller than 3).

In the latter, case, all the sub-groups are essentially having the same perception, as reflected in the *overall* percentage of favourable individuals, viz., P. If this value of P is greater than 10% it is concluded that the group as a whole is considering the item as important. If instead, this overall proportion is less than 10 per cent the conclusion drawn is that though some sub-groups show a proportion larger than 10 per cent this excess is possibly due to chance only and, all the sub-groups holding essentially the same perception, the item is considered not important by the group.

(vii) An illustration of calculating Z is given below, taking the figures in respect of the value Statement 'Duty'; which were as follows in the case of the Student respondents.

AF	AN or (n_1)	RF	RN or (n_2)	Total	AP or (np_1)	RP or (np_2)	Z
11	70	16	197	267	0.15714	0.08122	1.80981

Explanation of the above abbreviations

AN (or n_1) = Total number of respondents in the sub-groups accepting a particular value as important. The number of respondents in the sub-groups which favoured this value was 70.

AF = Actual frequency or number of respondents in the sub-groups constituting AN, who selected the value as important, 11 out of 70 had included this value in the list of ten important values.

RN (or n_2) = Total number of respondents in the sub-group(s) in which at least 10% of the respondents did not select the value and thus are considered to have rejected this value.

RF = Frequency of respondents in the RN sub-group(s) who opted for the value, through the sub-group(s) as such had rejected the value.

AP (or p_2) = $\frac{AF}{AN} = \frac{11}{70} = .1571$. In other words it is the proportion in the sub-group accepting the value.

RP (or p_2) = $\frac{RF}{RN} = \frac{16}{197} = .812$. It is the proportion in the sub-group rejecting the value.

PP (or P) = $\frac{AF + RF}{AN + RN} = \frac{16 + 11}{70 + 197} = \frac{27}{267} = .101$

This is the proportion in the total population of respondents.

Q = 1-P = which is 1 – .101 = .899

This is the proportion in the total population of respondents not accepting the value.

$$Z = \frac{p_1 - p_2}{\sqrt{PQ\left(\frac{1}{n_1} + \frac{1}{n_2}\right)}}$$

$$\text{or} = \frac{p_1 - p_2}{\sqrt{P(1-p)\frac{(n_2 + n_1)}{n_1 \times n_2}}}$$

$$\text{or} = \frac{.157 - .081}{\sqrt{(.101)(.899)\left(\frac{267}{70 \times 197}\right)}}$$

$$\text{or} = \frac{.076}{\sqrt{(.0909)(.0194)}}$$

$$\text{or} = \frac{.076}{\sqrt{.00176}}$$

$$\text{or} = \frac{.076}{\sqrt{.042}}$$

$$= 1.809$$

3. Broad Inferences

Based on the above, it was found that the respondents had graded certain values as important and certain values as not important. The former are indicated in Tables IA and IB and the latter in Tables II A to II E.

(i) (a) It would be observed that the following 12 values given in Table IA were considered important either on the basis of unanimity between the two groups, unanimity in one group and consensus in the other group, consensus in both the groups or consensus in one group and divided support by sub-group in the other group.

1. Discipline
2. Self-confidence
3. Proper utilisation of time
4. National consciousness
5. Good manners
6. National unity
7. Obedience
8. Punctualilty
9. Honesty
10. Cooperation
11. Duty
12. Friendship

(b) In the case of the following 8 values listed in Table IB, it is observed that though in each of these cases, at least 10% of the respondents in one of the main groups had favoured these values, there was sharp inter-se cleavage of opinion between the sub-groups. These values are:

1. Abstinence
2. Cleanliness
3. Dignity of manual work
4. Loyalty to duty
5. Patriotism
6. Secularism and respect for all religions
7. Sense of social responsibility
8. Value for national and civic property

(ii) Tables II A, to II E list Value-Statements which were not favoured by at least 10% respondents by any of the groups, hence these can be deemed to have been considered unimportant by the respondents.

(a) Table II A lists 27 values, which were not considered important by any of the sub-groups of the respondents.

(b) Table II B has 15 values, which were unanimously rejected by one of the groups, and rejected on the basis of consensus by the other group, or rejected by consensus by both the Groups.

(c) Table II C contains 6 Values not considered important by the General Population unanimously or by consensus; but considered important by one or more sub-groups in the Student Population.

(d) Table II D gives the list of 13 values not considered important by the Student Population unanimously or on the basis of consensus; but rated important by one or more sub-groups in the General Population.

(e) Table II E has one value, namely 'Quest for knowledge; which was not supported by at least 10% of the respondents in either of the groups and where there was sharp polarisation of views among the sub-groups in both the groups.

For studying the details, reference is invited to the relevant Tables in Appendix I.

Discipline

The statement reproduced below was included in the questionnaire to grade some of the causes of the prevailing indiscipline in the country.

"The following factors are responsible for indiscipline in the country—

a) Weakness of the administration
b) Trade Unionism
c) Game of politics" (G-17)

Grading Factors Responsible for Indiscipline

S.No. Factors	Name of persons who allotted Ist, IInd and IIIrd Positions to the Statements (a), (b),&(c)				
	Ist Position	IInd Position	IIIrd Position :	No. of Persons who expressed no opinion	Weighted Score
1	2	3	4	5	6
(a) Weakness of the Administration.	337 (38.2%)	293 (33.3%)	127 (14.4%)	124 (14.1%)	1011+586+127 =1724/2643 = 65.2%

1	2	3	4	5	6
(b) Trade Unionism.	74	175	507	125	222+350+507 = 1079
	(8.4%)	(19.9%)	(57.5%)	(14.2%)	= 40.8%
(c) Game of Politics.	351	285	118	127	1053+570+118 = 1741
	(39.8%)	(32.4%)	(13.4%)	(14.4%)	= 65.9%

(i) It would be seen that politics was considered as the first culprit for indiscipline in the country. This verdict is in consonance with the one indicated by the respondents in the case of statements G-8 and G-16, which have already been discussed in Chapter-II.

(ii) Close to this, the weakness of the administration is held responsible for indiscipline in the country.

(iii) Trade Unionism, as a factor responsible for indiscipline, is far behind these two factors.

National Unity

There was one statement in each of the questionnaires meant for general public and students having a bearing on national unity, to which the reactions of the respondent were invited.

Statement : " Political parties, to a great extent, are responsible for intersectional disharmony in the country."

(G-11)

The over-all picture in this case is given below:

Number Agreeing	Number Undecided	Number Dis-agreeing	Number of persons who expressed no Opinion
811	43	26	1
(92.1)	(4.9)	(2.9)	(0.1)

There was a high degree of agreement by all the sub-groups of the General Population with this statement, the maximum being from the advocates (100%) and college teachers (male)- 98%.

Promoting National Unity

The students were asked to grade the following factors in order of importance for promoting national unity.

Statement : In order to promote national unity, the following steps are desirable—

(a) Inter-caste marriages

(b) Each State should explore measures to provide jobs (work) to persons from other Indian States.

(c) Each State setting up a department to plan and implement programmes for national unity. (S-13)

Grading Factors Helpful to Achieving National Unity

S.No.	Factors	Number of students who assigned Ist, IIrd and IIIrd positions to these factors :				
		Ist Position :	IInd Position :	IIIrd Position:	No. of persons who expressed no opinion.	Weighted Score
(a)	Inter-caste Marriages (267)	84	107	73	3	67.3%
(b)	Policy regarding provision of work (267)	61	86	117	3	58.9%
(c)	Setting up of special departmental units (267)	119	72	73	3	71.6%

The respondents assigned first place to the setting up of separate departments for devising and implementing programmes which would promote national unity, evidently to give such programmes, a planned and a sound footing.

Inter-caste marriages was assigned second place among the three factors given in the statement. Narada Smriti mentions two kinds of marriages:

(a) Marriage between members of the same caste;

(b) Marriage where husband and wife belong to different castes.

The latter kind of marriage was further classified into two groups:

(i) **Hypergamous :** Where male belonged to a higher caste than the female;

(ii) **Hypogamous :** Where the woman was of a higher caste and male of an inferior caste.

Inter-caste marriage, therefore, must have been prevalent in ancient India. However, marriage within the caste was deemed better and in the case of inter-caste marriages hypergamous marriage was preferable to a hypogamous one. The present situation in India demands that the caste factor should be eliminated from the national life from as many spheres as possible by incentives or punitive measures, including social pressure.

As regards part(b) of the statement (S-13), perhaps no planned action has been stipulated either by the State governments or the Union Government in this regard. In order to promote inter-state mobility, which will contribute to national unity, some steps can be easily identified. For example, domicility condition, now prescribed by some States for jobs and admissions to higher educational institutions, should be relaxed. State governments should undertake on a big scale translation of classics and other works existing in various Indian languages into their respective languages. This would result in better understanding between different linguistic groups besides increasing the frequency of inter-state mobility because of the economic amelioration that such a programme would offer.[6] In fact, if this step had been taken some decades ago, even the language problem of the country would not have caused as big a threat to the national unity as it did by pro Hindi and anti Hindi violent demonstrations.[7]

It would be appropriate to briefly mention here some of the steps so far taken by the Federal and the State Governments to promote national integration.

The Central Government set up a National Integration Council which first met on June 2 and 3, 1962, under the Chairmanship of Jawaharlal Nehru, the then Prime Minister of India. The membership of this council consisted of the Prime Minister of India, several Union Ministers, Chief Ministers of States, representatives of political parties, educationists, trade-unions' representatives, persons from business, industry etc., Commissioner for Linguistic Minorities and Commissioner for Scheduled Castes and Scheduled Tribes. The second meeting of this council was convened on June 20 and 21, 1968. The then Prime-Minister, Smt. Indira Gandhi, chaired this meeting. At the second meeting, reports of the two groups which had been set up in 1962 were considered and accepted. These groups were:

(1) The Committee on National Integration and Regionalism

(2) The Committee on National Integration and Comunalism.

Some of the recommendations made by these two committees are summed up below:

1. Energetic development of Indian languages and literature.
2. Reaffirmation of the code of conduct which had been recommended by the National Integration Conference earlier.
3. Launching of National Integration Pledge from October 2, 1962. It has since continued year after year and is intended to promote national consciousness and keeping people away from violence.
4. Discouraging trends which keep minorities away from the national main-stream.
5. Keeping politics separate from religion.
6. According special concessions to those who marry outside their castes.
7. Dealing firmly with communal riots and taking strong action against administrators who err in this respect.
8. Creation of additional All India Services in forestry, medicine and engineering. The Constitution was amended in September 1963 to implement this proposal and the first Forest Service examination was conducted by the UPSC in 1967.
9. In order to ensure sovereignty and integrity of India, Article 19 of the Constitution was amended by Constitution (Sixteenth Amendment) Act, 1963, imposing reasonable restrictions on the freedom of expression. This was done on the recommendation of the Committee on National Integration and Regionalism.
10. Promotion of developmental programmes in the South to eliminate the feeling prevailing among certain sections that the South had been neglected in this respect.
11. Adoption of the national flag rather than individual flags by various political parties as their party-flags.

It is not a subject of this study to comment on the extent of implementation and success of these recommendations.The number of communal riots in the country, for some years, before and after the National Integration Conference of 1961, was as follows :[8]

Year	Number of Riots
1960	26
1961	92
1962	60
1963	61

Efforts so far made to achieve national and emotional integration of the country have not borne the desired fruit. There were several attempts for the political unification of the country since the Ancient Period, but these successes were unfortunately,shortlived.

"-------- From 3rd century B.C. to the 6th century A.D., India had run through two successive empires uniting India — The Maurya and the Gupta — but imperial unification had fizzled out by the end of the Gupta Period. The reunification under Harsha (606-647) was almost contemporaneous with China's reunification under the Sui dynasty but Harsha's effort was a swan song."[9]

Sankara established 'Maths' in the four corners of the country at Badri-Kedar in the Himalayas, at Dwarka in the West, at Puri in the East and at Mysore in the South with an eye on the cultural unity of the country. The prayers addressed to the seven sacred cities and seven sacred rivers have the same intent.[10] However, still much remains to be done. Educational Institutions, voluntary organisations and ministries like that of Information and Broadcasting can do a lot to remove political, social, economic, religious and other factors causing inter-sectional irritants and thus help in the process of bringing about national unity. Some of the programmes undertaken by different organs of the Union Ministry of Information and Broadcasting are mentioned below:

(a) *The All India Radio and the Doordarshan*

(1) The regional radio stations cater to the regional linguistic, cultural and other needs. The programmes such as the National programmes of talks, music, dramas, serials from Indian history, sangeet sammelans, symposia of poets etc. organised by the All India Radio & the Doordarshan centrally promote national unity.

(2) Broadcasting Hindi lessons from non-Hindi radio stations and lessons in regional languages from the Hindi radio stations.

(3) Annual organisation of the National Solidarity Day, on October 20.

(4) Featuring plays and programmes related to great men of India.

(b) *Publication Division and the DAVP*

The Publication Division and the Directorate of Advertising & Visual Publicity (DAVP) have been printing books, booklets and pamphlets on themes concerning various facets of Indian unity. The merit and useful of their material, however, need to be evaluated.

(c) *Field Publicity*

The Directorate of Field Publicity, in its programmes, specifically concentrates on the border areas of the country to break their isolation from the rest of the country.

(d) *Films Division*

The Films Division of the Ministry has produced several films like 'Land and the people of India'. 'Women in India', 'Let's sing Together', 'Jai Jawan', 'Unity — call of the Hour', 'South India', 'Sarvapalli S. Radhakrishnan' etc. to further the cause of Indian unity.

Social Service

The questionnaire for students contained the following statement on 'Social Service':

" Students should do social service among rural, tribal and backward people during a part of their long vacation". (S-5)

Students and Social Service

S.No.	Category of Respondents	Number Agreeing	Number Undecided	Number Disagreeing	Number of persons who expressed no opinion
1	2	3	4	5	6
(1)	Total Student population	230	23	13	1
	(267)	(86.1)	(8.6)	(4.9)	(o.4)
(2)	School students (M)	51	11	7	1
	(70)	(72.9)	(15.7)	(10)	(1.4)
(3)	School students (F)	81	3	2	0
	(86)	(94.2)	(3.5)	(2.3)	(0)

1	2	3	4	5	6
(4)	College students (M)	29	3	2	0
	(34)	(85.3)	(8.8)	(5.9)	(0)
(5)	African college students (M)	6	1	0	0
	(7)	(85.7)	(14.3)	(0)	(0)
(6)	College students (F)	63	5	2	0
	(70)	(90)	(7.1)	(2.9)	(0)

Notwithstanding the fact that social service was not assigned a high rank in the list of values (Table-II), there was, generally, a high degree of agreement to the statement. The girls, who are believed to have much greater spirit of sacrifice and a spirit of service agreed with the statement more than the boys did. Even the least agreement to the statement was 72.9 per cent which was from the school students (male). It is reported that in the United States of America, 45 per cent of the citizens do voluntary work in their spare time, averaging 4.7 hours per week.

" If these volunteers were paid at a rate of 10 per hour, the value to the economy of their combined work would be around 150,000 million per year—popular areas of voluntary work include assisting the elderly and the handicapped, assisting a paid employee of a public service organisation, baby-sitting, fund raising for charitable organisations, participating in a committee, serving as a coach, acting as a teacher or tutor, acting as a youth group-leader, serving an aide to a clergyman and volunteering in the arts. [13]

In the USSR, a programme of social service, called Subbotnik, is organised by the Central Trade Union of the USSR on a country-wide basis. This programme commenced on May 10, 1919 and Lenin himself also participated in this programme. Now the programme is organised regularly on a country-wide basis. According to official figures, annual output by production through Subbotnik is, of the order of several thousands of Soviet Roubles. The income thus generated is used for welfare and developmental work. Some of the projects already undertaken with this income are: The Cancer Research Centre in Moscow, Cardiological Centre in Kuebshev, Municipal Hospital in Kaza, Youth Palace in Moscow, Research Centre on Agricultural Problems in Siberia and Far East near Novosbirsk and Pioneer Camps and Health Camps etc.

A developing nation like India needs such a programme very badly. Therefore, it is time that India also launched on one such programme. In the Rigveda (VII. 79.2), God has been described as the God of Social Service," clothing the naked, curing the sick, making the blind see and the cripple walk about", Hindu religion enjoins on every one to perform 'Atithi Yajna', which is nothing but service of all human beings.

Kindness to Animals

Since long past, India has been recognising the importance of animals in the scheme of universe. In order to emphasise the importance of animls in human affairs the Puranas, which are combination of ethics, history and fiction, mention that of the many incarnations of God, some were in the animal forms such as of fish, tortoise, boar and narsimha (man-lion). The vehicle for the goddess Durga is said to be the tiger and that of Lord Ganesha a rat. Garud is the conveyance of Lord Vishnu, Swan of goddess Saraswati, buffalo of Yamraj, owl of goddess Laxmi and ox of Lord Shiva.

Ahimsa, which means no injury in thought, word and deed to any life form is a seminal concept in Hinduism and the concept was further developed by Buddhism and Jainism. Jains are very strict in regard to saving life. At some places, Jains have built hospitals for birds and beasts. "At Surat (Gujarat - India), there was till quite recently (1924)— a house where a host of noxious and offensive vermin, dense as the sands on the sea-shore were bred and nurtured; and at Anjar in Kutch, about five thousand rats were kept in a certain temple and daily fed with flour, which was procured by a tax on the inhabitants of the town."[15] There are, however, some religions which present a different thinking in this regard. For example, in Zoroastrianism, it is a heinous sin to kill one of Ormuzd (good) animals and pious to kill one belong to Ahriman i.e. harmful to man. The Greek thinkers from Socrates downward have no value for kindness to animals.

"In Siam tameness of many living creatures, which in Europe fly from the presence of man, is very striking. Instances have been known in which natives have quitted the service of Europeans on account of their willingness to destroy reptiles and vermin, and it is not an uncommon practice for rich Siamese to buy live fish to have the merit of restoring them to sea."[16] On this issue, the twentieth century Indian apostle of ahimsa, Mahatama Gandhi, said in his autobiography, " We are helpless mortals caught in a conflagration of *himsa*. The saying that life lives on life has a deep meaning in it. Man cannot for a moment live without consciously or unconsciously commiting outward *himsa*. The very fact of his living, eating, drinking and moving about — necessarily involves some himsa, destruction of life, be it ever so minute. A votary of ahimsa, therefore, remains true to his faith if the spring of all his actions is compassion, if he shuns to the best of his ability the destruction of the tiniest creature, tries to save it, and thus incessantly strives to be tree from the deadly coil of himsa. He will be constantly growing in self-restraint and compassion but he can ever become entirely free from outward himsa."[17]

In view of the importance of this value in our life the following statement was included in the questionnaire for students having a bearing on this aspect of the value-system.

"Rasool and Gian Kaur were discussing about kindness to animals. Rasool held that one should be kind even to creatures which are harmful to human kind. Gian Kaur felt that no kindness should be shown to beings like mosquitos, poisonous reptiles and dangerous creatures. Whom do you agree with?

(a) Rasool, whose concept of kindness included kindness to all animals;

(b) Gian Kaur whose notion of kindness excluded beings harmful to man. (S-7)

The opinion of the respondents to the two alternatives is given below:

Kindness to Animals

Option	No. of persons agreeing	No. of persons disagreeing	undecided
(a)	80 (29.9)	2 (.8)	
OR			11 (4.1)
(b)	172 (64.4)	2 (0.8)	

Thus, the respondents largely seemed to be favouring the philosophy of Zoroastrians in this regard.

Even if one were to favour the view that it is justified to kill animals harmful to man, one cannot justify the nailing of live snakes to trees for skinning, causing slow death to frogs after chopping off their legs, letting an animal die and stink on the roads because after all it is an animal only, starving the domestic animals or perpetrating cruelties on animals on any account.

Bhut Yajna

In this back-drop, one can appreciate the value and importance of bhut-yajna (worship of all life) listed as one of the maha yajnas in Hinduism. Kindness to animals emerges from the following sources:

(a) Superstition that the souls of killed animals would haunt the killer.
(b) Conviction that same life permeates all living creatures and that if an act of himsa is painful to human-beings, it is like-wise painful to animals also.
(c) Belief in the transmigration of soul.
(d) Intrinsic love and compassion for animals.
(e) Recognition of the usefulness of animals in human affairs.

The educational institutions can easily emphasise some of the aspect listed above, particularly the last one. There are about 500 varieties of animals, big and small, in India. Some of these are not found anywhere else in the world. As such they are a rare wealth of human race on this globe. According to an estimate, India has more than 20 per cent of the world's bovine population — nearly one half of the world's buffaloes and one sixth of the world's goat population, yet the milk production in India is only 6 per cent of the world's production of milk.[18] This is due to our indifferent or even unkind attitude towards animals. Disseminating proper and accurate information among all sections of the society in regard to animals is essential. Take the example of snakes. There are 216 species of snakes in India, out of which 52 varieties cause toxic symptoms in man.[19] Students and general public need to be educated on the shape, size and behaviour pattern of the poisonous varieties of snakes. Or at least about those which are commonly found in India and have more toxity in their bite so that they can guard themselves against such varieties and befriend with the remaining 164 varieties. It is a matter of common knowledge that snakes prefer rat-food. As such, they can, play a very useful part in rodent-control. Population of rats in India has been calculated at more than 8000 million and it is estimated that cereals worth thousands of crores of rupees which could feed lakhs of starving Indians is destroyed by them. The old custom of snake-worship by some people in India, in August-September of the year, must have been primarily designed as a ritual for thanks-giving to the snakes for their usefulness to man.

Goeth said; "Kindness is the golden chain by which society is bound together." We need to expand our vision to bring within the periphery of human-society birds, beasts and plants and all that nature has created and without which human society would cease to exist.

Subjective Ethics

All the foregiving values, however, need to be internalised. In any social set-up, both objective and subjective ethics are necessary. To the extent we succeed in promoting social conscience, the work of solving social problems becomes easier.

Super-Ethical Values

According to Indian belief, the highest ideal of life is the quest for ultimate Reality - the Brahman or the Cosmic Energy and the Moksha - attainment of freedom from the sufferings of the world. The Rishis advise that this can be achieved by pursuing the following path.

a) tapas - sacrifice or spiritual combustion;
b) adhyayana - quest for revelatory knowledge ; and
c) dana i.e., dedication/charity.

A person searching for super-ethical values maintains his link with the world of humans.through dana. As such, even when an individual is engaged in the quest for super-ethical values, total break with the material world is not recommended.

References and Notes

1. Crawford S. Gomwell, *The Evolution of Hindu Ethical Ideals*, The University Press of Hawaii, 1982.p. 130-151
2. *VESUDHA MANUSMRITI*, Aarsh Sahitya Prachar Trust, 1986, p. 228 (176/58).
3. The story of Satyakama is described in Chandogupanisada (4.4.4--Vs.5) Satyakama had approached Gautama Rishi to become his disciple. The Rishi, as customs obtained those days, asked the boy his family background. The boy, making a candid confession said;

" I do not know this, sir, of what family I am. I asked my mother. She answered me," In my youth when I went about a great deal as a maid-servent, I got you. So I do not know of what family you are. I am Jabala by name and you are Satyakama by name". So I am Satyakama Jabala, Sir".

Given such a truthful reply, the teacher responded: None but Brahmana could thus explain. Bring the fuel, my dear, I will receive you as a pupil. Thou hast not departed from the truth."

4. *VESUDHA MANUSMRITI*, Aarsh Sahitya Prachar Trust, 1986. p. 285, (92/62).
5. Ruhela S.P (ed), *Human Values and Education*, Sterling Publishers Pvt. Ltd., New Delhi 1986, p. 131.
6. See Appendix to the questionnaire given at the end.
7. Documents on Social, Moral and Spiritual Values in Education, National Council of Educational Research and Training, New Delhi, 1979, pp. 55-56.
8. Gandhi K.L., *The Problem of Official Language in India*, Arya Book Depot., New Delhi, 1984, pp. 49, 113.
9. Ibid, pp 53-72.
10. Gopal Krishna, The Times of India, New Delhi, December 28, 1988, p.6. For riots on the Language Issue in 1967, see The problem of Offical Language in India, p.66.
11. Subramaniam V. *Cultural Integration in India*, Ashish Publishing House, New Delhi, 1979, pp, 29-30.
12.(a) Names of seven sacred cities : Ayodhya, Mathura, Hardwar, Kasi, Conjeeveram, Ujjain and Dwarka.
(b) Names of seven sacred rivers: Ganga, Yamuna, Godavari, Saraswati, Narmada, Sindhu and Kaveri.
13. The Hindustan Times Evening News, New Delhi, December 26, 1988, pp1 and 22.
14. Westermark Edward, *The Origin and Development of the Moral Ideas*, Macmillan and Co. Ltd., London 1924, p. 499.
15. Ibid, p. 498.
16. See (Comp and ed) Borchert Donald M and Stewart David, *Being A Human In A Technological Age*, Ohio University Press; Athens, Ohio, 1979, p. 141.
17. Harbans Singh, *Domestic Animals*, National Book Trust of India, New Delhi, 1966, p. VII (Introduction).
18. Smith, M, *Fauna of British India, Vol. III*, 'Serpents', 1943. Deoras, P.J. *Snakes of India.*
19. Deoras P.J., *Snakes in India*, National Book Trust of India, New Delhi, 1981, pp. 1-5.

8

Social Justice

Social justice, as an objective of state policy, has been emphasised in the Indian Constitution. The preamble to the Constitution states :

> " We, The people of INDIA, having solemnly resolved to constitute India into a Sovereign Socialist Secular Democratic Republic and to secure to all its citizens Justice— social, economic and political; _____ "

In the list of 84 values appended to the questionnaire social justice was mentioned as one of the values. The following statement, having a bearing on this value, was included in the questionnaire for the general population and the people were asked to respond to the statement:

" In Indian Society, social justice is denied to women". (G–5)

Women and Social Justice

Sl. No.	Category of respondents	Number agreeing	Number Undecided	Number disagreeing
1	2	3	4	5
1.	Total population of respondents. (881)	586 (66.5)	106 (12.0)	189 (21.5)

1	2	3	4	5
2.	Male respondents (671)	395 (64.0)	65 (10.5)	157 (25.5)
3.	Female respondents (264)	190 (72)	41 (15.5)	33 (12.5)

It is, thus, seen that 72 per cent of female respondents felt that social justice was denied to them whereas 64 per cent of the male respondents subscribed to this view.

Human physiology and culture play an important part in determining the role of men or women in the group. Biologically speaking, man is larger in size and also sturdier than woman. Besides, woman has to bear and nurse children, which are bound to keep her indoors more than men. These factors determine different kinds of role for men and women and, to some extent, bestow dominant position to males.

The Vedic people accorded a respectable status to woman. The Vedas and the Puranas picture the female as divinity. She is worshipped as Adi Shakti (First creator), in the form of Mother Parvati and destroyer in the form of Kalika. Many great Grama Devatas (village gods) of south India — Mariamma, Elamma, Gangamma, Bhadrakali, Pida — are women. The names of the seven magic drugs and vegetables given in the Agni Purana and which are to be placed within amulets for ensuring victory over the enemies, are female — Mahakali, Chandi, Varahi, Isvari, Indrani, Vala and Gauri.

Indian women, in ancient days, did not lead a secluded life which circumstances forced on them in the later period. Women had the privilege of receiving high education. The custom of upanayana of girls prevailed down to the Sutra period.[1] Several Vedic hymns were composed by female Rishis. Some of the women, who composed vedic mantras are Apāta, Ghosā, Lopmudra, Indrani and Sarsvati still have a great influence on the Hindu society. Women like Sita, Ahaliya, Draupadi, Tara, and Mandodri are respected by both men and women alike even today. At a meeting of theologians convened by the scholar-king Janaka of Mithila, Gargi carried on a lively discussion with the great saint Yajnavalkya till she had extracted the definition of Brahman from him.[2] Maitreyi, the wife of Yajnavalkya, was also well-known for her scholarship.

During the famous theological debate between Adi Shankaracharya and Mandan Misra on the interpretation of the Vedas and the Upanisads, in which the former came out victorious, it was Bharati, the wife of Mandan Misra, who acted as the judge. She had been educated at a gurukul in prayag and she was known for her scholarship. At a later stage, Bharati herself had a debate with Adi Shankaracharya who was considered as one of the greatest masterminds of the Hindu philosophy.

The importance of female education is shown by the fact that according to the Atharva Veda, an educated brahmcharini had better prospects for marriage than one who was uneducated. Girls were then not married at an early age. In a hymn in the Rigveda (X,85, 21-22), the god of marriage, Visvavasu, is asked to go to a maiden who has attained the sign of marriage, whose body is developed and unite her to a suitable husband. The well-known ancient practice of Svayamvara indicates that women had a say in selecting their life partners. Widow-remarriage was allowed. A hymn in Rigveda (X, 18.8) says, "Rise up woman, thou art lying by one whose life is gone. Come to the world — and become the wife of one who is willing to marry thee." In religious ceremonies, wife had to be always by the side of her husband.

All this indicates the high position that women enjoyed in the Vedic India, though there are some contradictory assessments about the place of women in the society in the subsequent periods. Yajnavalkya and Vatsyayana give a positive assessment of the female character, whereas Dharma Sutras, Dharma Sastras and the Mahabharata, at places, adopt uncomplimentary view of women. In Ram-Charit-Manas, the great poet Tulsidas says that a drum, an uncultured person, an animal and a woman deserve to be beaten. The great Codifier of the Hindu laws, Manu, says, "— The gods reside where women are respected -----"[3] He also says," In childhood a woman must be subject to her father, in youth to her husband, and in old age to her son; a woman must never be independent because she is innately as impure as falsehood, the Lord created woman as one who is full of sensuality, wrath, dishonesty, malice and bad conduct". Vasistha says, "A teacher (acharya) is ten times more venerable than a sub-teacher (upadhyaya), the father a hundred times more than the teacher, and a mother thousand times more than the father".[4]

During the medieval period of Indian history, a considerable change took place in the status of women. "Widow remarriage was forbidden. The position of women was not as high as in ancient India — In a word, her (woman's) life was in a state of perpetual wardship — the Shastras laid down that the woman was socially and spirituallly inferior to man. The position of women worsened during the period of the Sultanate of Delhi,— The institution of the devadasis, in principal temples, was then in existence. Al-Beruni says that the priests were opposed to the institution of devadasis (beautiful maidens in temples practising devotional music and dance), but the kings, for the sake of revenue, maintained them even when it had degenerated in character."[5]

Vacillation or Evolution of Status

Naradsmriti, written after Manusmriti, permits niyoga, gambling as an amusement for women as it was for men, widow-remarriage etc. Similarly, there are several new features in the Brahaspatismriti and Katyayana Smriti. Brahaspati argues that when wife is half portion of her husband when he is alive, how anyone else can have a claim over husband's property when he is dead. There cannot anything more favourable to womanhood and more democratic in character than the Indian Shiva concept of Godhead itself being represented as a union of half-female and half-male, called Ardhnari-ishwara. Brihatsamhita, written by Varahamihira in the sixth century AD, declares, "Tell me truly what faults attributed to women have not been practised by men. — Women are superior to men who heap abuse on women who are pure and blameless". One may say that the Hindu view of woman has been vacillating between idealising and down-grading her; or one can also call it as varying with different law-makers and evolving with time and circumstances.

Status In Different Societies

A brief view of woman's status in ancient times in different societies, as described by Watermarck, would help us to arrive at considered judgement in regard to the status of Indian women.

"Among the East African Wanika a woman is a toy, a slave in the very worst sense; indeed she is as though she were a mere brute."[6]

Around 479 BC, the Chinese philosopher Confucius wrote,"------(A woman) is subject to the rule of three obediences. When young, she must obey her father and elder brother; when married, she must obey her husband; when her husband is dead, she must obey her son".[7]

A Chinese sayings describes, "Brothers are like hands and feet. A wife is like one's clothes. When clothes are worn out, we can substitute those that are new. When hands and feet are cut off, it is difficult to obtain a substitute for them."[8] Another saying has it," The best girls are not equal to the worst boys".[9]

Christian religion enjoins a husband to love his wife as his body, to do honour to her as unto the weaker vessel. However, man is not of woman; but the woman of the man. Neither was man created for woman; but the woman for man".[10]

Islam does not give equal status to women although it treats all men equal. The prophet is reported to have said," I have not left any calamity more hurtful to man than woman— assembly of women, give alms, although it be your gold and silver ornaments, for verily ye are mostly of Hell on the Day of Resurrection."[11]

Customs as Indicators of Status

It may be difficult to predict about the status of women on the basis of certain customs prevailing in the groups to which these women belong, yet it may be useful and interesting to allude to some of them.

" In North-West-Central Queensland, the women, on special occasions, are allowed to inflict punishment upon men; at a certain stage of the initiation ceremony each woman can exercise her right of punishing any man, who may have ill-treated, abused, or'hammered' her, and for whom she may have waited months or perhaps years to chastise."[12]

Among the Bakongo, a man would be much ridiculed by the women themselves, if he wanted to help them in their work in the field. Sometimes, agriculture is supposed to be dependent for success on a magic quality in women , intimately connected with child-bearing."[13]

In Abssinia, "it is infamy for a man to go to market to buy anything. He cannot carry water or bake bread; but he must wash clothes belonging to both sexes, and, in this function, the woman cannot help him."[14]

Notwithstanding the customs and rituals mentioned above, there is hardly any room for doubt that in ancient times, women in India enjoyed better status than their counterparts did in other societies.

Causes of Downfall in Status

Some of the causes leading to the lowering of social status of Indian women, through the corridors of time, are as follows:

(a) Even in the Vedas, there are prayers for the replacement of daughter by a son in the mother's womb, for it came to be held that parents attained salvation only through oblation by the son.
(b) Non Aryan females of low social classes were admitted into Aryan homes as wives and concubines. Aryans did not consider them fit for a high social status and gradually this led to the downfall in the status of all women.
(c) Polygamy contributed to lowering the status of women.
(d) Economic dependence of women on men assigned the former an inferior place.

Factors Contributing to Improvement in Status

With the spread of education and new ideas, the status of women has undergone a considerable change in many parts of the world. The movement to this end started during the Second World War which pulled out women from homes to manage cranes, shop-floors and other services. In the *Story of Civilisation*, Will Durant says (p. 131)," Until 1900 or so woman had no right which a man was legally bound to respect----. The emancipation of woman was an incident of the Industrial Revolution —. They (women) were cheaper labour than men; the employer preferred them as employees to more costly and rebellious males. A century ago in England, man found it hard to get work; but placards invited them to send their wives and children to the factory gate —."[15]

Woman's charm and grace is even now employed to promote business. Therefore what we interpret as an exercise for woman's freedom and equality was, to begin with, altogether a different thing.

In India, the freedom struggle, in which women participated in large numbers, as well as influence of the West, contributed greatly in ameliorating the status of women.

To some extent the welfare programmes, but largely the developmental activities-dissemination of education, training women for different vocations etc., will have an abiding influence in improving the status of women.

The Exploited Sections

In India, the status of women varies from class to class.

Generally speaking, in the upper strata of society, where people are better educated and there are no economic problems, women have considerable freedom and aspire to be equal with men. Among the working-class, tribals and agrarian societies, women are as good wage-earners as men, therefore they are, perhaps all over the globe as much privileged or handicapped as men and this is the group with the largest numerical strength in India. In the middle class, the position is different. A Bengali young widow may not be allowed to eat her staple food fish; but there is no such restriction for a widower. Among Muslims, man may divorce his wife; but the wife can not divorce her husband. If a girl is raped, the society is unwilling to accept her for marriage; but if a boy had a pre-marital or extra-marital sex experience, the society compromises with the situation more easily.

While all this may be true, the other side of the coin should also not be lost sight of. One of the post-graduate teacher respondents to the questionnaire wrote," Man is a victim of exploitation (by women). Cruelty and affliction is no longer a male sport. Education, freedom, economic independence have brought about a great change in the attitude of women and their treatment of men. There are many ways in which women can disrupt matrimonial life like bringing up false charges such as harassment for dowry by the in-laws, ill-treatment and torture from the husbands etc. Other methods could be nagging the husband, showing indifference to him and cruelty to children".

There exists an all-India organisation 'Akhil Bhartiya Patni Atayachar Virodhi Morcha' (All India Front for Prevention of Cruelties by Wives) which is demanding adoption of suitable laws for the protection of men from the atrocities of women. The Delhi Chapter of this organisation, in its meeting in Tis Hazari Courts in October, 1988 resolved," life has treated them (men) badly and there should be a law to protect hapless husbands from the wiles of women."[16]

The Reservation Issue

There was a statement in the questionnaire for students, which touched upon economic and cultural justice (and in a wider sense on social justice as well). It runs as follows:

"Reshma and Sunderrajan were debating continuance of reservations for scheduled castes and scheduled tribes in engineering and medical colleges. Reshma supported this practice whereas

Sunderrajan was against it. What do you think would be the right course for future?

(a) Reservations of seats in these institutions should continue;

OR

(b) Reservations* should be on merit alone.

(S-8)

Reservation of Seats in Professional Institutions

Sl. No.	Group	Persons agreeing option (a)	Persons agreeing option(b)	Un-decided	persons disagreeing option(a)	persons disagreeing option(b)
1.	School Students (M) (70)	9 (12.9)	60 (85.7)	1 (1.4)	-	-
2.	School Students (F) (86)	10 (11.6)	75 (87.2)	1 (1.2)		
3.	College Students (M) (34)	5 (14.7)	29 (85.3)	- -	- -	- -
4.	African College Students (M) (7)	6 (85.7)	1 (14.3)	- -	- -	- -
5.	College students (F) (70)	1 (1.4)	66 (94.4)	1 (1.4)	2 (2.8)	- -
6.	Total Population of Students (267)	31 (11.6)	231 (86.5)	3 (1.1)	2 (0.8)	- -

A glance over the above table would reveal that students preponderately opposed the idea of reservation of seats in professional institutions. Lack of support to the idea of reservations can emerge from several considerations. Firstly, institutions for professional training, in a way, pave a way to various job opportunities. Jobs are further related to the economic well-being of the country and managing positions of public responsibility in both case great care is needed. For example, if one is having a health problem, one

* The word should have been 'admissions' instead of 'reservations' here. In the Hindi version of the questionnaire, it was printed correctly.

would like to get treatment from the best possible medical practitioner, rather than one who owes allegiance to any particular caste or religion irrespective of his competence. This does not mean that persons belonging to SCs and STs have low merit. The Chairman of the Drafting Committee of the Indian Constitution, Dr. B.R. Ambedkar, was a scheduled caste mahar. The Writers of the Ramayana and Mahabharata also came from the scheduled castes. Balmiki was originally a bhangi and Vyas was born of Satyawati who was a daughter of a boat-man and a chamar by caste. Merit is no monoply of any particular group. However, it is necessary that adequate provisions should be made for those sections of society who have been educationally left behind so as enable them to make up the lee-way as quickly as possible. Many among the scheduled castes and the scheduled tribes feel that the provisions of reservations has not benefitted them as much as the element of discrimination against them by higher castes has harmed them. Therefore, today there is a great need for removing discrimination against them, wherever it exists. Lastly, some people are of the opinion that reservation policy should have been founded on economic backwardness and not on the basis of castes.

Constitutional Position

Articles 15(1) and 29 (2) of the Constitution of India, reproduced below, originally did not stipulate any discrimination between various citizens.

"Article 29 (2)

No citizen shall be denied admission into any educational institution maintained by the State or receiving aid out of State funds on grounds only of religion, race, caste, language or any of them."

"Article 15 (1)

The State shall not discriminate against any citizen on grounds of religion, race, caste, sex, place of birth or any of them.

"Article 15 (3)

Nothing in this article shall prevent the State from making any special provision for women and children."

However, the following addition was made in Article 15 of the Constitution (First Amendment) Act, 1951:

"Article 15 (4)

Nothing in this article (i.e. article 15) or article 29 shall prevent the State from making any special provision for the advancement of any socially and educationally backward classes of citizens or for the Scheduled Castes and the Scheduled Tribes.

Obliteration of Caste Barriers

There is no denying the fact that for a long time, low castes in the Hindu society were given a very harsh and a raw deal. For example, in southern Travancore, one mark of respect to the superiors was a bare breast. The priests honoured the deities in this way. By the same token, lower castes women were not allowed to cover their breasts. It was only in 1829 that the government of Travancore allowed the lower -caste women to cover their breasts, but not in the manner of higher caste Hindu women. Higher caste and lower caste Hindus used different language; as for example diferent words for water. Such things are, of course, now vanishing.

Rudolphs states that the following factors are gradually obliterating the caste differences in India :

"Four processes are making Indians more alike, and, in doing so, are laying the necessary but not sufficient conditions for national integration; ascriptive boundaries are expanding; the culture and the status of the twice-born varnas are spreading to Sudra castes; Westernisation is effecting the ideas and occupations of broader sections of society; and secularism is dismantling ritual barriers and disarming sacred sanctions."[17]

Due to progressive legislative measures, expanding educational facilities, gradual improvement in the economic status of scheduled castes and the scheduled tribes, people belonging to the so-called higher castes and lower castes tend to meet on equal terms. Also on account of the mobility of many people from villages to cities, where the caste origins of people are unknown, caste considerations are getting diffused.

Paradox

Paradoxically, certain scheduled castes now strive to retain their identity and would not allow higher castes to join them. "For example, in 1956 the chamars of Rajasthan were eager to disassociate themselves from their customary trade of leather working. By 1963, however, because of generous government financial and technical support to an industry capable of earning desperately needed foreign exchange and because of the advent of appreciable technical upgrading in the work involved, chamars were straining to exclude 'opportunists' from invading their ancient monoply."

Curricular Content

On the issue of social justice to women and SCs and STs, the following units may be considered for inclusion in the curricula for schools and colleges. Preparation of exhaustive curricula for different age groups suiting their mental age is left to the specialists.

(1) Broad picture of the present status of women in various sections of the Indian society and existing legislation on the subject.

(2) Status of women in ancient and medieval India.

(3) Female infanticide, malnutrition of females, rapes, dowry deaths, overburdening girls with household jobs etc.

(4) Emancipation of women in India and abroad.

(5) Developmental programmes which can ameliorate the status of women.

(6) The story of caste-system in India and how the system has been abused by the society.

(7) Social and economic injustice meted out to the SC's and ST's.

(8) Steps so far taken to improve the lot of deprived sections of society.

(9) Steps taken in other countries to improve the lot of people belonging to backward sections in their respective lands.

It hardly needs to be emphasised that every member of society should get economic, political and social justice, irrespective of class, caste or sex considerations.

Reference and Notes

1. *The Cultural Heritage of India*; Rama Krishna Institute of Culture, Calcutta 2nd ed, Vol.1, 1958; p.222

2. Pramatha Nath; *Epochs of Civilisation*; Asian Educational Services, New Delhi ; pp 126-127.

3. *Vesudha Manusmriti*; Aarsh Sahitya Prachar Trust, (Commentary Prof. Surrendra Kumar) ed, Rajiv Shastri), 1986 ; p. 184 (56/36).

4. Crawford S. Gomwell; *The Evolution of Hindu Ethical Ideals*; Asian Studies Programme, University of Hawaii, 1984; p. 68.

5. Srivastava M.P.; *Society and Culture in Medieval India*; Chugh Publications, Allahabad , 1975, p. 98.

6. Watermarck Edward; *The Origin and Development of the Moral Ideas*, Macmillan and Co., Limited, London, 1924 (Vol. I, II) ; p. 630.
7. Ibid, p. 648 (Legge, Chinese Classics, r 103 sq.).
8. Ibid p. 648 (Indo-Chinese Gleaner, I. 164).
9. Ibid, p. 662.
10. Ibid, p.654 - (Corinthians, XI 8 sqq).
11. Ibid, p. 662 (Lane-Poole, Speeches of Mohammad) pp. 161, 163.
12. Ibid, p. 631 (Roth Ethnol, Studies Among the North -West - Central Queenland Aborigines, pp. 141- 176).
13. Ibid, p. 637.
14. Ibid, p. 636.
15. Mutahhari Murtada; *Rights of Women in Islam*, World Organisation for Islamic Services, Tehran, Iran, 1981s; preface, xxx.
16. *The Times of India*; October 26, 1988, Section 2, p.3.
17. Rudolph Lloyd I and Rudolph Sussane Hoeber; *The Modernity of Tradition*, University of Chicago Press, Chicago, London, 1969; p. 111.
18. Ibid, p. 134.

9

Protection of Environment

The world, it seems,, is steadily drifting towards its doom by rapidly exhausting its natural resources. speaking on 'Sustainable Development of Natural Resources' at the 76th Science Congress, the well-known Indian scientist Dr. Swaminathan said, "Nature's patience is not inexhaustible and we have tested it too much already. Unless political leaders, professionals and the public worked in concert as members of a symphony orchestra, sustainable development would remain an elusive goal."[1]

Depletion of resources

The following statement pertaining to consumption of natural resources was included in the questionnaire for general public.

"The present generation is excessively consuming natural resources such as minerals, oils, forests etc. which is unfair to future generation." (G-7)

The response-pattern is shown in the following table:

Excessive consumption of Natural Resources

Group	Number Agreeing	Number undecided	Number disagreeing
Non-student general category of respondents	615 (69.8)	91 (10.3)	175 (19.9)

Natural resources include soil, water, air, energy, forests, flora and fauna, living aquatic resources and minerals etc. Some of these resources such as solar energy and ocean energy are inexhaustible; forests are renewable whereas fossils and mineral resources are non-renewable.

These resources get depleted in the following ways:

(a) *Normal Utilisation:* Natural resources are consumed by human beings to meet life's needs. Increasing population in the country is adding to the existing heavy load on our resources. In order to conserve resources, it would be necessary for all sections of society to control population. Government has implemented Family Planning programme to arrest the trend of fast increasing population, yet the problem of over-population stays and the burden on our resources continues.

(b) *Excessive Utilisation:* The present generation seems to be over -utilising the natural resources. Commercials advertisements prompt modern man to consume more and more. Man seems to be living for this moment only, as if secretly realising that tomorrow he might die.[2] Gandhiji said, "Earth has enough for every man's need, but not for every man's greed".

Importing material from abroad is also not a workable proposition to make up for the shortage of resources. Take the example of crude oil. According to a report, India imported 22 million tonnes of crude oil in 1987-88, which was 22% more than the import of 1986-87. The import of crude oil touched 24 million tonnes in 1988-89 i.e., it was up by another 9 per cent in the subsequent year. Thanks to the fall in the prices of oil in 1988-89, that the burden on the country's exchequer did not increase; but even then for a country like India, with serious economic and foreign exchange limitations to pay foreign exchange to the tune of Rs. 4,000 crores a year for import of crude oil is not something which should be viewed lightly. And this expenditure has been looking upwards since then. The solution, therefore, lies in exercising a strong check on consumerism.

(c) *Unscientific Utilisation:* Sometimes, resources are wasted when these are not used scientifically or are not recycled, wherever this is possible.

(d) *Pollution:* Resources are wasted due to pollution also. Whereas industrialisation and mechanisation have contributed to economic prosperity, they are greatly responsible for water, air, noise, chemical and biological pollution as well as accumulation of hazardous industrial waste.

(i) *Water Pollution*: Water pollution is mainly being caused by industrial and sewage waste flowing into the rivers and the lakes. Several rivers in the country have got pollution and acquatic life-forms subsisting on these waters are in danger of getting annihilated. The dumping of nuclear waste into the oceans also poses similar dangers as well as of mutilating the species living in the oceans.

(ii) *Air Pollution*: Automobiles are among the biggest culprits in polluting our physical environment. It is estimated that in the cosmopolitan cities of India, 60% of the atmospheric pollution is due to gases emitted by unburnt fuel of the automobiles. The unburnt fuel emits hydro-carbons, oxides of nitrogen, carbon monoxide and carbondioxide.

Carbonmonoxide, which is colourless and odourless, is lethal when present in the air in the ratio of 4:100. Moreover haemoglobin in the blood has 240 times more affinity for absorbing carbonmonoxide as compared to absorbing oxygen. In other words, distribution of this gas in the atmosphere is like administering the people a form of slow poison.

Hydro carbons, oxides of nitrogen give rise to respiratory problems, irritation in the eyes and several other health problems. The content of these gases and subsequent hazards to our health increase manifold if automobiles emit more unburnt petrol or deisel.

Inspite of these dangers, the number of automobiles is annually rising by millions in the country. If mankind is to be saved from this pollution, number of automobiles will have to be restricted by making public transport more efficient and devising other suitable measures.

Depletion of ozone-level in the atmosphere has been going on due to emission of chlorofluorocarbons (CFCs) by increasing the use of refrigerators, air-conditioners and aerosol sprays. Advanced countries of the world are more responsible for it than the developing nations. For example, America uses nearly 30 per cent of world's CFCs as against India and China which together are using about 2 per cent of CFCs.

There is also evidence that in the Arctic Region, which had been pollution free, ozone-destroying form of chlorine is hanging all over now. In the Antarctic, ozone, loss has already occurred due to man-made chlorofluorocarbons. With the loss of the ozone-layer, the ultra-violet rays of the sun would reach the earth causing skin diseases and cancer etc.[3]

(iii) *Chemical and Biological Pollution*: Use of chemical fertilizers and pesticides effects mankind in two ways. Firstly, the surface of crop-lands is damaged and secondly pesticides sometimes find their way into the human system. Researches have shown presence of DDT in hen eggs. Not long ago, India imported sizeable quantity of chlorodane, a highly toxic substance, from the United States. The USA banned its use in their country because it was found to cause cancer in animals but India continued to import this pesticide.

Another bizarre import was of harmful coal power plants (on hefty price) from Saarland in West Germany where these plants had been shut down, and virtually become a scrap, following protests by environmentalists and medical experts.[4]

Burning of chemicals and suffocating materials release toxic substances (which effect blood), virus and bacteria etc.

(iv) *Noise Pollution*: Increasing transport and expanding industries, lead to noise pollution. Noise pollution is reported to cause many physical and psychological ailments such as headache, fatigue, hypertension, sleeplessness, deafness, and other disorders. According to W.H.O., 45 db is the safe noise limit. 'Noise' is nearly on top of the agenda in all regular meetings of the WHO. It has been estimated that the three cosmopolitan cities of India have over 90db on non festival days and much more than this on the festival days. It is said that it takes 20-50 hours of quietitude to combat the 'ill effect of the noise caused by four hours of a rock concert. Round the clock radio and television programmes and addiction to pop and hi-fi loud music are adding further to noise pollution. This is why some commercial firms, in highly industrialised countries, have silence-rooms where the workers can retire and unwind themselves by being away from the noisy atmosphere.

(v) *Industrial Waste*: This is yet another source of enviornmental pollution. The highly industrialised Western nations which have fully benefitted from the fruits of industry are now worried about the disposal of the industrial waste. These (wealthy) nations have signed contracts with ten African countries —Congo, Equitorial Guinea, Gabon, Guinea Bassau, Nigeria, Senegal, Sierra Leone, Guinea and Benin[4] —where industrial waste would be dumped. Obviously, it is a case of rich nations criminally exploiting the poor.

New Imperatives:

There may be some divergence of views in regard to the causes of excessive dilapidation of the natural resources but there can be hardly any difference on the point that the country needs to utilise its limited natural resources wisely, otherwise the consequences would be far too serious. Industrial man has to fall in line with the environmental imperatives and redefine his strategies of progress (economic), production (of consumer goods), population (growth) and pollution (by industrial waste and otherwise).[6]

"Lack of regard for environmental factors helped destroy the great civilisations of the Middle East, in the Tigris and Euphrates valleys, and in Jorden. Their demise is history. To the deforestation and over-grazing of the past, man today has added air pollutants at levels which inhibit photosynthesis, he has introduced oxygen-using chemical agents into lakes, streams and aquifers; he has released insecticides, herbicides, and radioactions, and he has covered millions of acres of garbage, spoil and mining gangue."[7]

Striking a note of optimism, Dr. Whitfield wrote, "We are an ingenious and adaptable species and we have the power to destroy life on our planet, we have perhaps the wisdom to save it. We are engineering the planet, whether we like it or not, so we had better do it well, controlling our own growth, limiting our greed and getting back to ways of life that can be sustained indefinitely."[8]

Environmental Education

Environmental education would include education from, about and for environmental. Broadly speaking, India has three eco-systems- The Himalayan Ranges, the Indo-Gangetic Plains and the Tropical Rain Forests. The content of environmental education would include some general elements for all students and some specific aspects pertaining to these three systems. Regarding general elements of environmental education, students can be educated on following lines:

(a) Nature is a great inspirer of art and literature. The sensitive mind of Wordsworth could observe 'tongues in trees and books in running brooks'. Writers, thinkers, philosophers, saints, time and again, take refuge under nature's canopy and come out physically, intellectually and spiritually enriched. Some scholars hold that the Aryans compiled their Vedic literature in the natural environments near river Saraswati, that is why they named the goddess of learning after the name of this river. Such great is the contribution of nature to our civilisation and culture.

Learning about environment means understanding about the meaning and importance of ecological balance, role that nature plays in sustaining life, richness and diversity of replenishable and non replenishable natural resources and so on.

Learning for environment aims at developing love and

respect for things of nature—living and non-living — and protecting them from damage and pollution. It was not without meaning that trees and animals were worshipped in ancient India. Elements of nature were looked upon as gods. Thus, concern for environment is nothing new. Of course, in recent times this concern has become multi-dimensional because our problems have become more complex. Our forefathers did not pollute the Ganges and other rivers and they held them sacred; today we clean them in the name of having a pollution - free environment.

Malaysia has developed a syllabus on environment which is worked out around the following six themes. The scope and depth of these themes increases in the educational curricula from year to year.

(i) Child and his surroundings.

(ii) Interaction among man i.e., human relations.

(iii) Interaction of man with his environment.

(iv) Interaction of elements in our environments

(v) Issues related to man.

(vi) Issues related to environment.

The National Council of Educational Research and Training New Delhi, has also worked out a syllabus for environmental education.

Global Awakening

For some time now there has been world -wide awakening in regard to the environmental issues. The United Nations Organisation convened a conference on environment at Stockholm in 1972. It focussed attention on the dangers to human life posed by continuous degradation of the eco-system. It was followed by the Belgrade Charter of 1975; Inter-governmental meet at Tbilisi in 1977, and International Conference on Environmental Education in New Delhi.

The Globala Perium held a five-day conference in Moscow in January, 1990 to focus the attention of delegates from all over the world on 'Environment and Development for Survival'. The conference was inaugurated by the U.N. Secretary General and concluded with an address by the President of the USSR. The 1972 Stockholm Conference recommended that the Secretary General, the organisations of the United Nations System especially UNESCO should "take necessary steps to establish an international programme in environmental education (IEEP), interdisciplinary in approach, in school and out of school encompassing all levels of education and directed towards the general public, in particular the ordinary citizen living in rural and urban areas, youths and adults alike, with a view to educating him as to the simple steps he might take, within his means, to manage and control his environment".[9]

The Indian Parliament passed the Constitution (Forty-Second Amendment) Act, 1976 for safeguarding the environment. This legislation, which became a part of the Directive Principles of State Policy, is as follows:

"Article 48A

The state shall endeavour to protect and improve the environment and to safeguard the forests and wild life of the country".

Environmental Diplomacy

In recent times, many countries are trying to assume world leadership in holding conferences on protection of environment. In March 1989, the Prime Ministers of France and Netherlands called a meeting of 24 countries in Hague to discuss environmental problems. America kept away from this meeting. The British Prime Minister, Ms Margaret Thatcher, convened on her own a meeting of 123-nations on measures to protect the ozone layer of the earth. This inspired America to convene another meeting to debate global environmental issues.

All nations are, today, worried over the increasing greenhouse effect such as of carbon-dioxide etc. on the environment. As a result of greenhouse gases (GHGs), the universe is experiencing changes in temperature and getting warmer, rainfall pattern is changing and sea-levels are rising. Consequent to rise in sea-level, the islands of Maldives and parts of India and Bangladesh are threatened by getting sub-merged under water. Therefore, the world has to search for new models of development rather than following the old models. Preservation of resources and saving the atmosphere from pollution should be treated as a matter of highest concern rather than a sphere of diplomacy or a hunting-ground for leadership. The world community must choose between balanced economic growth and annihilation; between international rivalaries and cooperation; between carefully preserving the resources or wrecklessly exhausting them.

India's call at the summit meet of the Non Aligned Movement in Belgrade on September 5, 1989 had a great wisdom in it. The

Indian Prime Minister suggested raising of an 18 billion dollar international Planet Protection Fund' for saving the globe from further environmental degradation. India had proposed at the conference that each country developed or developing — should contribute 0.1 per cent of its GDP for this purpose. This fund, which should be monitored under the UN auspices, could be used for reforestation, stemming of floods, population control, checking ozone depletion and the greenhouse effects and many other programmes which could save resources on the globe from pollution and extinction.

Conclusion

Though the Vanmahotsav, the Chipko Movement and the opposition generated against the Narmada Project (in Gujarat) are indicators of public awakening in India on environmental issues, yet a holistic and energetic approach for conservation of natural resources, compatible with the gravity of the problem, is yet to emerge. Public mind needs to be made more alive to the dangers posed by denuding of forests, pollution of water and other resources, especially the non-renewable resources. In the Union of Soviet Socialist Republic, near the city of Bratask, there is a forest where timber is estimated to last for 100 years. As and when the trees are cut in this forest, new trees are planted. By the time the existing trees are utilised, new trees would have grown in their place, as such this forest would last 'for ever'. A good model to emulate!

If the voice of reason is not heeded to and adequate steps are not taken betimes to protect natural environments, Asia would suffer for the sins of Europe, Africa for the sins of Australia, Arctic and Antartica for the sins of the United States of America and vice-versa. Lord Buddha had said, "Many a time, it is not our own sins but the sins of the others which envelop and destroy our inner repose and outer surroundings". Therefore, a coordinated and an integrated approach is called for on environmental issues by the world-community. To borrow the words of Dr. Karan Singh, Indian prince, politician and a scholar, "it is left to us if we would convert this beautiful planet into a burnt cinder or will cherish her as a cradle for higher consciousness. Mankind would do well to remember the following note of wisdom and caution which he sounded at the Global forum. "We live in a shrinking world in which old traditions of conflict and competition will have to make way for the new culture of convergence and cooperaton if the rich-promise of the next millennium is not to evaporate in a thermo-nuclear inferno."[10]

References and Notes

1. Dr. Swaminathan. The Hindustan Times, New Delhi, January 9, 1989, p. 10
2. Wheelder Harvey (ed). *Beyond the Punitive Society,* Operant Conditioning, Social and Political Aspects, W.H. Freeman and Company, San Francisco, 1973, pp. 57-70.
3. *The Times of India,* New Delhi, June 7, 1988, Section 2, p. 8.
4. The Statesman, Delhi, September 12, 1989, *Poison and Pollution,* p.6.
5. *Wake Up India;* (News and Trends), July-September 1988, The Vasanta Press, The Theosophical Society, Adyar, Madras, p.30.
6. Wheeler Harvey (ed); *Beyond the Punitive Society.* pp. 57-70..
7. Becht J.E. and Belzung E.D., *World Resources Management* Prentice Hall, New Jersey, 1975, p.x.
8. Dr. Whitfield, G.R., in *Human Values and Education,* ed. Ruhela S.P., Sterling Publishers Pvt. Ltd., New Delhi, Bangalore p. 142.
9. Desh Bandhu and Ramanathan N.L. (ed), *Education for Environmental Planning and Conservation,* Indian Environmental Society-Edited: Proceeding of the International Conference on Environmental Education organised by Indian Environmental Society and Department of Environment, 1982, p. 179.
10. Dr. Karan Singh (art) *Strengthening Global Consciousness;* The Hindustan Times (Magazine Section p. 9), January 21, 1990, New Delhi.

10

Modifying Human Behaviour

Article 51A of the Constitution (Fortysecond Amendment) Act, 1976, lays down the following Fundamental Duties. These may be termed as a value-system which the government expects every citizen of India to observe faithfully.

"Article 51A: It shall be the duty o1 every citizen of India —

(a) to abide by the Constitution and respect its ideals and institutions, the National Flag and the National Anthem;

(b) to cherish and follow the noble ideals which inspired our national struggle for freedom;

(c) to uphold and protect the sovereignity, unity and integrity of India;

(d) to defend the country and render national service when called upon to do so;

(e) to promote the spirit of common brotherhood amongst all the people of India transcending religious, linguistic and regional or sectional diversities; to renounce practices derogatory to the dignity of women;

(f) to value and preserve the rich heritage of our composite culture;

(g) to protect and improve the natural environment including forests, lakes, rivers and wild life, and to have compassion for living creatures;

(h) to develop the scientic temper, humanism, and the spirit of inquiry and reform;
(i) to safeguard public property anu to abjure violence;
(j) to strive towards excellence in all spheres of individual and collective activity so that the nation constantly rises to higher levels of endeavour and achievement.

Based on the study of the Gandhian literature and reports given by committees and commissions on social, moral and spiritual values in education, the National Council of Educational Research and Training, New Delhi compiled an exhaustive list of 84 values. given in the Appendix to the questionnaire.

It is difficult to make comparison of the moral standards between societies. Laws, rules, customs, opinions vary from society to society, from individual to individual and from time to time. Moral relativism is an eternal phenomenon.

Moral Relativism

According to ancient Indian scriptures, there are seven seminal concepts of values. These are rta (cosmic order); verna (class); asrama dharma (duties for different stages of life); law of karma (moral causation); samsara (transmigration); ahimsa (harmlessness); and moksha (liberation).

Indians have the unique distinction of producing and practising philosophical and ethical thought from very early days. "Unlike ethical teachings of ancient Egypt and Babylon, Indian ethics was philosophical from the start. In the oldest Indian writings, the Vedas, ethics is an integral part of philosophical and religious speculation about the nature of reality. These writings date from about 1500 BC*. They have been described as the oldest philosophical literature in the world, and what they say about how people ought to live may therefore be the first philosophical ethics."[1] Ancient Chinese regarded filial piety, reverence for the superiors, love of the past and exercising moderation as cardinal virtues. The ethical ideals of ancient Greeks were not influenced by theological considerations. They were more concerned with the duties of an individual as a member of the city-state. Christian-values like humility, meekness, gentleness, compassion and renunciation of

* According to the latest researches and evidences based on carbon dating of a copper head and the astronomical content of the Vedic literature, the Rig Veda would be older than 4000 B.C (1a, 1b)*

the world were held in disesteem by the Greeks as well as the Romans who were more inclined towards materialistic ideals.

Assessment of Moral Standards

Anthromorphic man today presents a picutre of a mechanomorphic man. There is a general feeling that the industrial man has gone far ahead of the moral man, hence, the present crisis in all our walks of life. On the contrary, people like Myers hold. In no domain has progress been greater, the gains larger or more precious, than in the moral domain. From clan morality, based on physical kinship, mankind has advanced or is advancing to world morality, based on ethical kinship of man. There appears not only a new physical but also a new moral man."[2] 88 per cent of the respondents to statement G-1 of the questionnaire felt that moral values among Indians have declined over the past 5-10 years. To a similar statement (S-4) that "Majority of Indians are selfish and lack dedication of ideals", students reacted as follows:

Dedication to Ideals

Sl.No. Category of respondents	Number Agreeing	No. Undecided	Number disagreed
1. Total Population of students (267)	140 (52.5)	42 (15.7)	85 (31.8)
2. School students (M) (7)	38 (54.3)	13 (18.6)	19 (27.1)
3. School students (F) (86)	51 (59.3)	15 (17.4)	20 (23.3)
4. College students (M) (34)	16 (47.1)	5 (14.7)	13 (38.2)
5. African College students (M) (7)	3 (42.9)	1 (14.2)	3 (42.9)
6. College students (F) (70)	32 (45.7)	8 (11.4)	30 (42.9)

Diversity of views on the subject notwithstanding, the nation, in general, feels that there is urgent need for elevation of moral standards in the country.

Determinants of Behaviour

For planning any programme of moral uplift, it is necessary to delineate the factors which influence human behaviour. Broadly speaking, some of the important determinants of man's behaviour are as follows:

(i) Religion and Science

According to religious people, most of our ills arise from inside ourselves; from desire, pride, lust, etc. For others, the ills come from external agents like poverty and natural disasters etc., and that we can overcome these external forces through technology and industrialisation. There is no denying the fact that both moral-health and material-progress are necessary for mankind's balanced progress.

Science at one time seemed to hold that religion was irrelevant and it was a creation of man's childish ignorance. Having achieved considerable success in science and technology, Europe, today, seems to be turning to East for discovering its spirit. And, surprisingly, Orient is getting lured by material progress of the west![3]

(ii) Nature, Nurture and Free Will

In cold regions, where struggle for existence is hard, life is lived more at the physical plane. That is why cultural growth is comparatively slower there and faster in warm, temperate and fertile regions. This also explains why the story of all conquests is the story of more civilised nations getting conquered by less civilised nations and thereafter the victorious being absorbed by their 'victims'.

The biological or the social environment is also important. Man has considerable influence on another man. The cultural influence of India over East and South East-Asia and that of Egypt on the West are testimony to this fact. The art of coining money and building temples in India is considered to have Greek influence. Conversely, Buddhism influenced the Gnostic Greek sects. "Numerous drugs of Indian origin are noticed by the Greeks — A variety of treatises on medical science were translated from Sanskrit into Arabic and Persian — The Saracens introduced the Indian method of Arithmetic and the Indian Algebra and Geometry into Europe."[4]

It does not carry conviction that human-beings perform their role in this world only at the bidding of fate or some providential force. The inherited genes, and according to Hinduism, the Samaskaras of previous life-cycle, no doubt influence our behaviour pattern, but the claim of nurture in human development cannot be undermined. The environmentalist, J.B. Watson, said in 1920, "Give me a dozen healthy infants, well formed, and my own specified world to bring them up in, and I will guarantee to take any one at random and train him to become any kind of specialist. I might select doctor, lawyer, artist, merchant, and, yes, even beggarman and thief — regardless of talent, penchant, tendencies, abilities, location, and race of his ancestors."

According to Toynbee heredity and environment alone can not explain all behaviour patterns. He says," I part company with the behaviourists over their belief that behaviour is wholly and exclusively determined by heredity and environment."[6] According to him, self-determination (or free-will as the Hindu scripture Gita puts it), has a good claim to be considered as one of the important determinants of human behaviour.

(iii) Materialism

Economic pulls, today, seem to be exercising a great influence on human kind. We seem to be drifting towards Machiavellian philosophy that the end of human existence is profit alone. When a man is dedicated to economics to the exclusion of laws of life, virtue no longer remains his prime concern.

Modifying Behaviour

Man's behaviour can be modified in two ways:

(a) By use of behavioural science and technology.

(b) Through the process of education.

(a) Behavioural Science and Technology:

Scientists have been doing considerable research on the modification of human behaviour in order to find ways and means to remove behavioural pollution.

(i) *Drugs*: It is learnt that leading nations are secretly engaged in what is known as chemical factors or behavioural drugs; for example drugs which can be sprayed over large population centres and which can make them docile in a manner so as to make the work or the invading armies easier.

(ii) *Foods*: It may be possible to achieve similar results (as by drugs) by proper kinds of foods. The type of food, its quantity as well as quality — all influence the physiology and psychology of living organisms. Therefore, by appropriate kinds of foods it may be possible to shape the desired type of individuals.

(iii) *Electronics*: Electronics provide another measure of behaviour control. Electrodes are implanted in the human brain so as to stimulate certain behaviour centres. The stimulation can be achieved by remote control also.

(iv) *Genetic Engineering*: This has made it possible to remove congenital defects and, in course of time, to engineer a human being of one's choice (good as well as bad).

(v) *Reinforcement and Aversive Stimuli* : Reinforcement is negative as well positive — i.e., removing certain things from the environment or adding certain things to it. One can escape from the consequence of fire either by fleeing it or removing the fire from the environment.

Punishment for undesirable behaviour is an aversive stimulus. It may have side effects also. For example, a prisoner may become more intrepid in the jail in the company of other prisoners and pick up more techniques of committing crimes. Motivating a person to do something by offering awards is a positive reinforcement. It has fewer side effects.

(vi) *Experimental psychology*: Considerable theoretical and experimental work has been done in the field of psychology — a science which deals with the functioning of human mind. This is becoming available to modern man for modifying individual's behaviour.

Some of the technologies described above are still a distant possibility and may not be available to mankind at least for immediate and large-scale application. Therefore one has, at the present juncture, to rely more on the educational process.

(v) *Educational process*:

(i) *Role* — Education is a major instrument in modifying human behaviour. In addition to the family, educational institutions have considerable influence on how individuals behave and function. It is, therefore, important that education — defined both in narrow and broader sense— concerned itself with educating the future generation in desirable values. Comenius and Locke described value-education as the hub of educational activity. "Indeed the term 'Humanities', as used to designate a very large section of the curriculum (for a long time, in fact, the whole of the curriculum) indicates by its derivation that relations between man and man were seen as the central, or even the only, concern of education in the full sense. Moral upbringing, or character training, therefore, was for long the central feature of what education itself was understood to be by the great theorists and, indeed, by great practitioners. —It was probably with the development of education for all and the concomitant introduction of a vocational component into the curriculum that moral education lost, in part, this central role."[7]

Moral education programme can be accomplished through educational institutions, religious institutions and the mass media. Whereas schools and colleges will impart moral education to students, religious institutions can be more usefully employed for inspiring the general public and mass media for both these groups to develop in the individuals propensity for higher standards of conduct.

(ii) *Personal Example:* Formal teaching can promote moral values only when children see that teachers themselves practise the code of conduct which they want their students to follow. In the case of moral education, it is necessary to have the marriage of thought and action. Action without thought is blind and is likely to degenerate into superstition; whereas thought without action is of no consequence. Teachers' training-programme should educate the individuals, both, in content and methodology of moral education.

(iii) *Proper Syllabus:* National Council of Educational Research and Training, New Delhi has worked out a syllabus on moral education. Some broad outlines in regard to syllabi on social justice, sex-education, smoking, drinking and protection of environment have been given in the foregoing chapters also. Certain schools in the country have made some ad-hoc provisions for imparting moral education to their students. An exercise done by the St. Xavier's Secondary School, Delhi for drawing up a syllabus in moral education may be seen in Appendix-II.

(iv) *Inter-disciplinary Approach:* Values concern all life-forms, birds, plants and even non life such as use of natural resources etc. Therefore value-education calls for an inter-disciplinary approach. The following episode would explain the usefulness of such an approach.

Once the residents of a housing complex complained to the owner of the housing complex that they had to wait for a long time for the lift. The owner called engineers to find a solution to the situation. One suggested fixing of an additional lift; the second replacement of the old lift by a new one; but the owner turned down these suggestions as costly. A psychologist happened to pass that way. He advised fixing of two mirrors in the waiting lounge, hoping that ladies would keep looking into the mirrors and arranging their hair etc. and men would keep looking at the ladies in these mirrors and thus waiting will become easy. The suggestion worked wonderfully well with a nominal expense.

(iv) Production of Literature

Another important work to be done in this area is the writing of suitable books suiting various age-groups of students. These books as text books or supplementary readers should emphasise the proud record of India's cultural heritage and lives of those who dedicated themselves to the service of mankind. A good deal of published material exists already also and can be used judiciously[8] for this purpose. Besides, import of foreign literature beaming with sex, violence and other unhealthy trends should be stopped.

Educational institutions and mass media have, no doubt, an important part to play in restructuring the moral fibre of the society, but it should be remembered that they are surrounded by a system which negates the promotion of moral values and makes their work difficult. Unless their difficulties are resolved, success would remain a distant goal. Further, it should be ensured that no dominant religious, caste, political or any other pressure group is allowed to promote values which serve its particular vested interests. The work is obviously not easy. The example of Vidur, the unflinching moral teacher in the Mahabharata Epic, is a proof of this statement. However, if adequate steps are not taken to implement the programme of value-education in right earnest, mankind may have to face serious consequences.

In the end, it may be added that in India—there is no dearth of ideas and philosophical thought, but unfortunately, most of the reports of research studies, workshops and committees or commissions find their place on the shelves of cold storage only. Preparation of such reports can, in a way be likened to marriages of elephants where everything takes place at high level; there is lot of trumpeting but nothing happens for (two) years. We need to be more realistic as well as practical. The world is moving fast. Our survival depends on our capacity to keep pace with the changing times.

Reference and Notes

1. Encyclopedia Britannica, Volume 18, 198. p. 630.
1a. H.H Hicks, R.N. Anderson," Analysis of an Indo-European vedic Aryan Head - 4th Millenium B.C." Journal of Indo-European studies, Vol. 18, 1990.
1b. B.G. Sidharth," Mahayuga : The Great-Cosmic cycle and the Date of the Rig Veda," B.M.Birla Science Centre (Hyderabad), Research Report, February 1991.
2. Myers, Philip Van NESS, *History as Past Ethics - An Introduction to the History of Morals*, Boston; GINN and Company, 1913, pp. 4-7.
3. Gilkey Langdon, *The Religious Dilemmas of a Scientific Culture — The Interface of Technology, History and Religion* (chapter IV) in Borchert M and Stewart David, *Being Human in Technological Age*, Chio University Press, 1979. p.
4. Bose, Pramatha Nath, *Epochs of Civilisation*, Asian Educational Service, New Delhi, 19 p. 48.
5. Yankelo ch David in Bochert M and Stewart David, *Being Human in a Technological Age*, Ohio University Press, Athens, Chio, 1979, p. 92.
6. Wheeler Harvey (ed), *Beyond the Punitive Society, Operant Conditioning*, Social and Political Aspects, W.H. Freeman and Company, San Francisco, 1973, p. 120.
7. Downey Meriel and Kelley A.V., *Moral Education; Theory and Practice*, Harper and Row, London, 19,p.10.
8. Virat Hindu Samaj, 15 Institutional Area Lodi Road, New Delhi-110003, has published a classified bibliography on 'Literature on Moral and Spiritual Values'. Bhartiya Vidya Bhavan, K.M. Munshi Marg, Bombay has also produced a good deal of useful material in this regard. Besides, considerable ancient literature like the stories of Panchtantra, the Epics etc. contain wealth of material which can be of considerable help in imparting moral education.

TABLE–1 A

VALUES CONSIDERED IMPORTANT EITHER BY THE GENERAL POPULATION OR THE STUDENTS OR BY BOTH THE GROUPS

S. No.	Value-statements	General population		Student population		Remarks and Inferences
		PP	Z	PP	Z	
1	2	3	4	5	6	7
(1)	Discipline (20)	17.48	-	36.70	-	All the 15 Sub-Groups—eleven in the General-population and four in the student—Population-considered this Value as important. There being no difference of the perception between the various Sub-Groups on the importance of this values the question of Z value in this case does not arise.
(2)	Self-confidence (63)	11.46	2.43	11.99	1.74	Z i.e., the measure of difference of perception within the Groups, being less than 3, it can be inferred that *on the basis of consensus,* both the Groups rated this value as important.

1	2	3	4	5	6	7
(3)	Proper utilisation of time (48)	10.22	2.22	17.23	-	All the four Sub-Groups in the student population unanimously considered this value as important. The General population, on the basis of consensus, accepted this value as important.
(4)	National consciousness (43)	14.42	-	6.37	2.59	Whereas in the General Population all the 11 Sub-Groups considered this value as important, in the student population the consensus was not in favour of this value. As such if National Consciousness is to be cultivated among students, suitable steps in this regard will have to be taken at the school stage as well as at the college stage. It is an example of generation gap in the perception.

1	2	3	4	5	6	7
(5)	Good manners (28)	6.92	2.16	26.22	-	Though all the 4 Sub-Groups of Students included this value among the important Values, in the case of the General population, the consensus was not in favour of rating the value as important. The two Groups perceive this value differently.
(6)	National unity (42)	14.76	2.81	6.74	1.27	In the General population group, there was consensus in favour of this value; but in the student population, the consensus was grading the value as not important. It is again a case of generation gap. In case the value of National unity is to be stressed, similar course of action will have to be taken in the case also as indicated above in respect of cultivating 'National consiciousness'.

1	2	3	4	5	6	7
(7)	Obedience (46)	-	-	19.85	2.61	There is wia variation between the views of the two Groups. The Students, by consensus, favoured this value, whereas none of Sub-Groups in the General population rated this value as important.
(8)	Punctuality (49)	6.24	4.52	17.23	1.83	The consensus of opinion among the Student Group considered this value important, but the General population respondents, by consensus, rejected this value.
(9)	Honesty (31)	8.29	2.43	13.11	2.13	Consensus of opinion among the students rated this value as important, whereas the General population perceived the value as unimportant.
(10)	Cooperation (7)	-	-	10.49	2.58	There is polarisation of perception in regard to this value. Students, by consensus favoured this Value, whereas the Sub-Groups in the General popula-

1	2	3	4	5	6	7
						tion unanimously rejected this value.
(11)	Duty (19)	7.60	3.99	10.11	1.81	Except for General population (Rural) and Doctors/Advocates, no other Sub-Group in the General population considered this value as important, whereas among the students there was a consensus in rating the value as important. If it accepted that 'Loyalty to duty' discussed below and 'Duty' are, more or less, overlapping values, then there is consensus among all the 15 Sub-Groups in rating this value as important whereas 17.86% of the Rural population considered it important, only 6.52% of the urban respondents considered it important.

1	2	3	4	5	6	7
(12)	Friendship (23)	-	-	10.11	1.33	Sharp polarisation of views among the two Groups is clear. Friendship is a strong urge during one's youth but this ideal seems to be waning as age advances. Further, among the students, it is interesting to note that whereas 12.18% of girls favoured this value, only 7.21% of boys favoured it.

TABLE–1 B

VALUES (ARRANGED ALPHABETICALLY) MARKED BY SHARP POLARISATION OF VIEWS WITHIN THE SUB-GROUPS OR BETWEEN THE TWO GROUPS

1	2	3	4	5	6	7
(13)	Abstinence (1)	11.69	3.88	13.48	3.99	Only the General population (female), General population (male) General population (rural) and primary teachers, School students (male), School students (female) favoured this value. the college students and Sub-Groups belonging to various professions did not vote for this value. Broadly speaking, the elite sections of the respondents did not consider 'Abstinence' as important.
(14)	Cleanliness (8)	-	-	12.36	3.04	The School students (female) and all Sub-Groups in the General population did not consider this value as important. Only 3.49% of School students (female) voted for this value.

1	2	3	4	5	6	7
(15)	Dignity of manual work (18)	10.10	4.15	-	-	The General population (female), General population (male) and General population (Rural) did not rate the value as important and none of the Sub-Groups among the students considered this value important. In the General population, whereas 10.61% of female voted for this value 9.89% of males—rated it as important. Considerable work will be required to be done in order to cultivate this value among students.
(16)	Loyalty to duty	13.96	2.48	10.11	3.88	Among the General population, there was a consensus that this value was important; but in the Student Group there was polarisation of perception among the school and the college students. Both the Sub-Groups (male and female) of college stu-

1	2	3	4	5	6	7
						dents did not regard this value as important. Whereas 15.38% of school students voted for this value, only 2.70 of College students graded this value as important. Therefore, this Value needs to be emphasised at the College stage in particular.
(17)	Patriotism (50)	13.5	4.51	7.87	1.97	Sub-Groups which did not consider this value as important are as follows: (a) Sub-Groups of students, on the basis of consensus. (b) Sub-Groups General Population (female), Defence personnel, Doctors/Advocates, Secondary School Teachers (Female) College Teachers (Female) and Educationists. It would be observed that the Student Group have not rated the values of National conscious-

1	2	3	4	5	6	7
						ness, National unity and patriotism as important. In case the society considers the cultivation of these values as important, considerable work needs to be done in this regard in the educational institutions. Another area causing alarm in this respect is that of the Defence personnel, even if the respondents in this Sub-Group were desk workers in the Defence Department.
18)	Secularism and respect for all religions (75)	11.12	3.10	-	-	Besides all the four Sub-Groups of student, the following Sub-Groups in the General population did not rate this Value as important. (i) General Population (Rural) (ii) Secondary School Teachers (female) (iii) College teachers (female) (iv) College teachers (male)

1	2	3	4	5	6	7
						Only 5.79% of respondents in the above four Sub-Groups favoured this value, whereas 13.15% of the respondents in the remaining Sub-Groups of the General population considered this value as important. In a multi-religious society, as India is, this is not a good sign that students and teachers do not consider this value as important.
(19)	Sense of social responsibility	10.44	3.17	3.0	4.75	The following Sub-Groups did not consider the value as important. (i) Except male college students, all the remaining 3 Sub-Groups of Students. (ii) General population (female) (iii) General population (rural) (iv) Primary teachers (v) College teachers (male) (vi) Educationists.

	2	3	4	5	6	7
)	Value for national and civic property (84)	15.55	3.28	5.24	5.22	In the General Population, the following 3 Sub-Groups did not consider this value as important. (i) Doctors/Advocates. (ii) College teachers (male) (iii) Educationists. In the Student Group, except the college students (female) no Sub-Group considered this value as important. When college teachers (male) did not rate this value as important, no wonder the college students (male) also do not attach importance to this value. If loss to national and civic property is to be prevented, it will be necessary to emphasise this value in the curricula of the educational institutions.

Note :- (i) (–) Shows, in all the Tables, Zero Value.

(ii) Figures under the Value-Statement indicate the serial numbers of these statements as given in the Appendix of the Questionnaire.

VALUES UNANIMOUSLY CONSIDERED NOT IMPORTANT BY THE GENERAL POPULATION AS WELL AS STUDENT POPULATION

TABLE : II A

S. No.	Value statement
1.	Anti-untouchability (3)
2.	Compassion (9)
3.	Common cause (10)
4.	Common good (11)
5.	Endurance (21)
6.	Equality (22)
7.	Faithfulness (24)
8.	Freedom (26)
9.	Gratitude (30)
10.	Helpfulness (32)
11.	Initiative (35)
12.	Kindness (38)
13.	Kindness to animals (39)
14.	Leadership (41)
15.	Purity (51)
16.	Resourcefulness (53)

S.No.	Value Statement
17.	Reverence for old age (56)
18.	Self-support (64)
19.	Self-restraint (68)
20.	Solidarity of mankind (70)
21.	Socialism (73)
22.	Sympathy (74)
23.	Spirit of enquiry (77)
24.	Team work (78)
25.	Team spirit (79)
26.	Truthfulness (80)
27.	Universal truth (82)

VALUES STATEMENT CONSIDERED NOT IMPORTANT UNANIMOUSLY BY ONE OF THE GROUPS AND BY CONSENSUS BY THE OTHER GROUP

TABLE: II B

S. No	Value-Statements (Alphabetically)	General Population		Student Population	
		PP	Z	PP	Z
1	2	3	4	5	6
(1)	Consideration for others (5)	3.97	2.73	-	-
(2)	Curiosity (14)	-	-	8.61	2.02
(3)	Devotion (16)	3.75	2.31	-	-
(4)	Gentlemanliness (29)	-	-	4.12	2.88
(5)	Hygienic living (34)	-	-	7.12	2.84
(6)	Integrity (36)	4.88	2.95	-	-
(7)	Justice (37)	4.43	2.91	-	-
(8)	National Integration (45)	6.47	2.80	-	-
(9)	Self discipline (60)	9.42	2.37	-	- 11.90% of Rural respondents and 9.16% of the urban respondents considered this value important
(10)	Self help (61)	-	-	5.99	2.33
(11)	Self-control (67)	7.04	2.94	-	-
(12)	Sense of discrimination between good and bad (72)	8.63	1.71	-	-

1	2	3	4	5	6
(13)	Universal love (73)	4.43	1.64		
(14)	Respect for others (55)	5.45	1.25	7.49	0.93
(15)	Sincerity (57)	4.77	2.40	9.36	1.77

VALUES NOT CONSIDERED IMPORTANT UNANIMOUSLY OR BY CONSENSUS BY THE GENERAL POPULATION; BUT CONSIDERED IMPORTANT BY ONE OR MORE SUB-GROUPS OF STUDENT POPULATION

TABLE : II C

S. No.	Value-statement	General Population		Student Population		Student Sub-Groups having marked perception in favour of the Value.
		PP	Z	PP	Z	
(1)	Fellow feeling (25)	-	-	5.24	3.33	College Students (Female)
(2)	Regularity (54)	-	-	8.61	3.07	School Students (Female)
(3)	Concern for others (6)	2.95	2.47	3.37	3.40	College Students (Male)
(4)	Courage (12)	6.36	1.91	9.36	3.67	College Students (Male) and College Students (Female)
(5)	Non Violence (44)	6.36	2.34	4.49	3.26	School Students (Male)
(6)	Social Service (69)	7.04	2.61	5.99	4.58	College Students (Female)

VALUES NOT CONSIDERED IMPORTANT UNANIMOUSLY OR BY CONSENSUS BY THE GENERAL POPULATION; BUT CONSIDERED IMPORTANT BY ONE OR MORE SUB-GROUPS OF STUDENT POPULATION

TABLE : II D

S. No	Value-Statement	General Population		Student Population		Sub-Groups in the General population having marked perception in favour of the Value
		PP	Z	PP	Z	
1	2	3	4	5	6	7
(1)	Appreciation of cultural Values of others (2)	7.26	4.73	-	-	Doctors/Advocates, Primary Teachers, Secondary Teachers (Female), College Teachers (Male), Educationists.
(2)	Citizenship (4)	6.81	3.13	-	-	General Population (Rural), Primary Teachers, Educationsits.
(3)	Courtesy (13)	3.06	4.64	-	-	Defence Personnel, College Teachers (Male)
(4)	Democratic decision making (15)	6.02	4.64	-	-	College Teachers (Male), Educationists.

1	2	3	4	5	6	7
(5)	Dignity of individual (17)	3.41	4.25	-	-	College Teachers (Male)
(6)	Forward look (27)	2.84	4.08	-	-	Primary Teachers
(7)	Peace (47)	2.61	5.27	-	-	Primary Teachers
(8)	Social justice (59)	2.04	4.10	-	-	College Teachers (Male)
(9)	Self respect (62)	5.68	4.07	-	-	Defence Personnel College Teachers (Female)
(10)	Self reliance (66)	6.24	3.09	-	-	College Teachers (Female)
(11)	Tolerance (81)	5.79	3.56	-	-	Defence Personnel, Doctors/ Advocates
(12)	Humanism (33)	5.79	3.86	7.12	2.04	Secondary Teachers (Female), Educationists
(13)	Self Study (65)	4.99	5.30	9.74	2.22	College Teachers (Female)

VALUE-STATEMENT WHERE SHARP DIFFERENCE OF OPINION WAS OBSERVED IN BOTH THE GROUPS

TABLE : II E

S. No.	Value-Statement	General Population		Student Population		
		PP	Z	PP	Z	
(1)	Quest for knowledge (52)	9.65	3.08	9.36	3.24	(a) Defence Personnel, Secondary Teachers (Female), College Teachers(Female), College Teachers (Male), Educationists (b) School Students (Male), College Students (Male)

APPENDIX–I

QUESTIONNAIRE

1. Value education i.e., education regarding discrimination between what is right or wrong, should be imparted in schools & Colleges.

2. Mahesh and Rakesh were exchanging views on smoking. Mahesh said that one should never smoke. Rakesh said that limited smoking for the sake of keeping company should not be looked down upon. Who in your opinion is right?

a) Mahesh, who totally opposes smoking

OR

b) Rakesh, who favours smoking within limits for the sake of company.

3. It is pardonable, if a needy person accepts bribe.

4. Majority of Indians are selfish and lack dedication to ideals.

5. Students should do social service among rural, tribal and backward people during a part of their long vacation.

6. Students should be made aware of Indian culture through history, literature and other books.

7. Rasool and Gain Kaur were discussing about kindness to animals. Rasool held that one should be kind even to creatures which are harmful to human kind. Gian Kaur felt that no kindness should be shown to beings like mosquitos, poisonous reptiles & dangerous creatures. Whom do you agree with?

(a) Rasool, whose concept of kindness included kindness to all animals.

OR

(b) Gian Kaur whose notion of kindness excluded beings harmful to man.

8. Reshma and Sunderrajan were debating continuance of reservations for schedule castes and schedule tribes in engineering and medical colleges. Reshma supported this practice, whereas Sunderrajan was against it. What do you think would be the right course for future?

(a) Reservations of seats in these institutions should continue.

OR

(b) Reservations should be on merit alone.

9. No stigma should be attached to sexual ralations before marriage.

10. Keeping in view the conduct of majority of Indian teachers, one concludes that their quality is-

(a) Of the desired level.

OR

(b) Average

OR

(c) Below the desired level.

11. Religious institutions such as temples, mosques, churches should play greater role in propagating moral values in the society.

12. Sex education should be imparted in-

(a) Schools.
(b) Colleges.

13. In order to promote national unity, the following steps are desirable.

(a) Inter-caste marriages
(b) Each state should explore measures to provide jobs (work) to persons from other Indian States.
(c) Each State setting up a department to plan and implement programmes for national unity.

14. The following factors are responsible for lowering the status of teachers

(a) Lack of scholarship in teachers
(b) Teachers' lust for money
(c) Absence of sacrifice among teachers for their students.

15. Young generation will show more respect to their parents, if

(a) Parents gives greater freedom to their children as children grow in age
(b) Parents spend more time with their children
(c) Parents themselves keep adjusting to changing social values.

16. From the appendix, list in order of priority five values for each stage of education. Please indicate in the brackets only the

serial numbers as given in the appendix of the values selected by you. Besides, if you so wish you may mention other values which you think are important; but these are not mentioned in the appendix.

APPENDIX-II

MORAL SCIENCE SYLLABUS

(Drawn up at Teachers' Workshop at St. Xaviers School on August 22, 1987)

SUMMARY OF DISCUSSIONS TO EVOLVE THE MAIN DIRECTION OF THE VALUE EDUCATION PROGRAMME OF THE SCHOOL (WORKSHOP I)

1. **PROBLEMS**

   Lack of integrity of character. Lack of concern for others. Selfishness. Lack of Social consciousness. Lack of respect for human dignity. Poverty. Cut-throat competition. Economic and Social disparilty - the widening gap. Lack of equality; of justice. Lack of a vision in life. Materialism. Lack of discipline.

2. **ROOT CAUSES**

   Materialistic Values. Cut-throat competition. Rich-poor gap. Corruption. Conscious and sub-conscious feudalistic attitudes. Superior-inferior complex. Inequality : division into the haves and the have-nots. Proper values are not imparted at home or at school.

3. **MAJOR THEME (the main direction to be developed by the programme)**

   Self-respect. Self-discipline. Respect for the dignity of every human being. Brotherhood. Equalilty. Dignity of labour. Need for a religious foundation in life; for prayer.
   The major themes can be understood as the expressions of *human growth* along three dimensions : *Personal, Spiritual* and *Social;*

PERSONAL

Self-discipline. Self-respect. Respect for human dignity. Freedom in the diverse spheres of human life.

SPIRITUAL

Spiritual growth, drawing from religious traditions. Prayer

SOCIAL

Struggling to remove the conditions of poverty for all; social consciousness. Respect for human dignity. Brotherhood. Equality. Justice.

SCHEME FOR VALUE EDUCATION

The syllabus for each class has three tracks (Topics from the tracks can be selected by the teacher according to the class 'needs.)

TRACK I : Values of Personal growth

TRACK II : Values of spiritual growth

TRACK III : Values of social growth.

STD VII

TRACK I

Know yourself; observation of one's own behaviour; its analysis.

Who am I ? What am I now?

Developing self-respect; awareness of self-growth, of one's uniqueness; self-confidence.

Developing a sense of responsibility; fearlessness (especially, telling the truth without fear); initiative; hardwork.

Promoting self-lessness, cooperative spirit, spirit of sharing.

Cultivating respect for property, one's own and that of others.

Imparting clear directions on cleanliness, punctuality, use of refined language, courtesy, proper manners, respect for elders.

Understanding home's contribution towards the development of the Young person — physical, emotional, cultural, spiritual.

TRACK II

Prayers based on situations in Tracks I and III. Exercises in being silent for a short period of time.

TRACK III

Know your surroundings; Visit slums, hospitals, orphanages, old people's homes; become aware of the needs of others.

Exposure to the great personages of India. The Freedom Movement.

Promoting civic sense; awareness of oneself as a member of a community; civic duties.

STD VIII

TRACK I

What I would like to be.

Awareness of one's strengths and weaknesses; of those of others.

Love of friends, class-mates, the not-so-fortunates.

Seeking to realise one's potentialities and talents; disciplined learning in academics, sports; cultivating the scientific temper.

Independent thinking (not blindly following others).

TRACK II

Prayer sessions based on situations in Tracks I & III.

Awareness of the good points in other religions.

Appreciating the views of others and their cultural traditions.

TRACK III

Knowledge of the Constitution; Our rights; duties; provisions to promote human dignity and justice.

Patriotism; national integration; builders of modern India.

Know your city; your State - Promoting equality and justice for all the citizens of the country.

ST. XAVIER S SCHOOL, DELHI

A SUGGESTED SCHEME FOR VALUE EDUCATION

The syllabus for each class (UNIT) has three tracks :

TRACK I - Myself - a fully human person.

TRACK II - With a mature relationship to the Transcendent.

TRACK III - And a serious commitment to society.

UNIT A

TRACK I - **WHAT IS A PERSON?**

I am a person - therefore unique
My qualities - good/bad; strengths/weaknesses.
My feelings - in general; emotion/love; urges, conflicts/complexes.

My gift of reason
My gift of - self-restraint.
free will - discipline/control.

The fully integrated person.

TRACK II - **THE SPIRITUAL DIMENSION OF MAN**

India's quest for the Supreme-Her spiritual heritage; Her great spiritual personalities.

Heed for a spiritual dimension in life— man's search for meaning-origin/mission/destiny.

The essense of a spiritual dimension—Belief in God and dependence on Him; Prayer and Worship.

TRACK III— **KNOW INDIA**

Her richness of culture/beauty/natural resources.

India marching ahead-Technologically/economically : educationally/socially.

India's Problems - poverty/ill health/overpopuation; illiteracy/un-employment.

Social reformers of India -B.R. Ambedkar; Mahatama Gandhi.

UNIT B

TRACK I- THE PERSON I AM

My attitudes to people-trust/distrust/respect/courtesy/prejudice
Work-dignity of labour/responsibility.
Possessions - greed vs. generosity.
Mass Media - consumerism vs. Service.
My Value;
My use of freedom
My relationship to - my family -consideration/cooperation/compassion. - my friends.

My self-image.

TRACK II- SPIRITUALITY/MORALITY TODAY

True and False Concepts of spirituality.
-Conformism/empty ritual/ignorance/tradition.
-Freedom vs. Compulsion/poor/family pressure.
-Materialism-Atheistic Rationalism /Agnosticism/Communalism/Sectarianism.
-Challenge of the Transcedental. My spiritual dimension.

TRACK III- ANALYSE INDIA

Society as it is social/economic disparity.
Society as it should be—Preamble to the Constitution; Fundamental Rights.
The causes of Social Injustice; Economic; Socio-cultural; Political;
Self-centeredness of man.
My contribution to the problem.

UNIT C

TRACK I- THE PERSON I CAN BE

Maturity — Freedom and responsibility.
Relationships in general—Relation with opposite sex : Commitment for life.
Making the right choices—Rationale of a right choice.
Problem solving/case studies.
The critical analysis of mass media.
My emergent self.

TRACK II- MY SPIRITUAL DIMENSIONS

Its benefits—Relationship with God; Values; Suffering;

Evil—as a discruption of relationship; Restoration of relationship Internal peace.

My response—a prayerful experience of gratitude/appreciation.

TRACK III-LOVE INDIA

Justice - its essence-respect for the dignity of all men as persons and sons of God.

Means to promote justice.

- Equal opportunity (education)
- Fundamental Rights and Duties
- Exercise of right Values.

Obstacles to Justice

- Indifference/lack of awareness/skills.
- Social pressures-human respect/ambition /prejudice /biases/favouritism/nepotism.

A Just Society.

UNIT D

TRACK I - THE PERSON I WILL BE

Obstacles-facing failures/human respect/peer groups/authority figure unrealistic self-image.

Means -Analysis of personality.
-Problem solving on actual personality problems;
-Self-acceptance; Independent thinking ; personal convictions.

My transparent self.

TRACK II-THE DEMANDS OF A MATURE MORALITY/SPIRITUALITY

An agent of Social reconstruction and change.

-Qualities needed

-Commitment; political consciousness

Choice of career-urban/rural/less lucrative/more lucrative/pressures conflicts.

My vision of Life - a man for others.

An Adult living in an unjust society, if he is to follow out his mature religious faith and be fully human, must be a committed agent for social change.

What is my basic option?

APPENDIX–III

JAPANESE MORALS RESCRIPT

"Know ye, our subjects :

"Our imperial ancestors have founded our empire on a basis broad and everlasting and have deeply and firmly implanted Virtue; our subjects, ever united in loyalty and filial piety, have from generation to generation illustrated the beauty thereof. This is the glory and the fundamental character of our Empire, and herein also lies the source of our education. Ye, our subjects, be filial to your parents, affectionate to your brothers and sisters; as husbands and wives be harmonious; as friends true; bear yourselves in modesty and moderation; extend your benevolence to all; pursue learning and cultivate arts, and thereby develop intellectual faculties and perfect moral powers; furthermore, advance public good and promote common interests; always respect the Constitution and observe the laws; should emergency arise, offer yourselves courageously to the state; and thus guard and maintain the prosperity of our imperial throne coeval with heaven and earth. So shall ye not only be our good and faithful subjects, but render illustrious the best traditions of your forefathers. [1]

"The way here set forth is indeed the teaching bequethed by our imperial ancestors, to be observed alike by their descendants and the subjects, infalliable for all agree and true in all places. It is our wish to lay it to heart in all reverence, in common with you, our subjects, that we may all thus attain to the sense Virtue.

"The 30th day of the 10th month of the 23rd year of Maiji" (1890).[2]

It would be almost impossible to exaggerate the influence of this imperial edict. "Our whole moral education," affirms Baron Kikuchi, "consists in instilling into the minds of our children the proper appreciation of the spirit of this rescript."[3]

---

1. Beron Kikuchi, in Sedler, Moral Instruction and Training in Schools (1908), Vol.ii,p.331.

2. Ibid, Vol, ii, p. 319.

3. Ibid, Vol, ii. P. 230.

INDEX